CRIMES THAT SHOCKED AUSTRALIA

Published by Brolga Publishing Pty Ltd
ABN 46 063 962 443

PO Box 452
Torquay Victoria 3228
Australia

email: markzocchi@brolgapublishing.com.au

National Library of Australia
Cataloguing-in-Publication data
Ian Ferguson, author.
ISBN 9781921221569 (paperback)

A catalogue record for this book is available from the National Library of Australia

Printed in Australia
Cover by David Khan
Designed and typeset by Imogen Stubbs

CRIMES THAT SHOCKED AUSTRALIA

IAN FERGUSON

ACKNOWLEDGEMENTS

I especially acknowledge the expertise of my wife Ann, who contributed the informative chapter titled "Crimes in a Technological Age" in this publication.

Ann, along with our daughters Belinda and Amy, also shared the exacting role of proof reading the text with our good friends Jeff and Helen Wallace, and I thank them all for their valued assistance.

Ian Ferguson (April 2008)

CONTENTS

CHAPTER ONE:

BUSHRANGERS OF VICTORIA'S NORTH-EAST

Australia has a long association with criminal history, as the first European colony established was a penal settlement. Convicts continued to be herded off sailing ships onto our shores for decades, well after Governor Arthur Phillip first raised the British flag on 26th January 1788, which is now celebrated as Australia Day.

Since those convict days Australians have continued to eulogise a variety of scoundrels. "Waltzing Matilda", a popular folk song about a sheep rustler who evades the law by committing suicide, is still regarded by many as being our unofficial national anthem.

Habitual criminals such as Ned Kelly, "Squizzy" Taylor and Mark "Chopper" Read are entrenched folk heroes to many. Michael Hodgeman, a former Federal Member of Parliament attended "Chopper's" marriage in Tasmania, and disgraced New South Wales (NSW) detective Roger Rogerson is much sought after for dinner speaking engage-

Roger Rogerson

ments. In 2007 ex-Prime Minister John Howard, and ex-Victorian Premier John Brumby, both expressed public support for the late billionaire businessman Richard Pratt, after he was charged with illegally forming a lucrative business cartel.

In contrast to these "celebrity" names, the criminal class of colonial times endured lives of grinding hardship. Co-existence between wardens and convicts was always volatile, and in 1856 growing tensions in the prison system erupted into violence. Ten convicts led by Thomas Smith, (alias "Captain Melville"), killed a guard, and escaped from the rotting hulk "Success" which had been their prison at Williamstown.

Ten convicts killed a guard, and escaped from the rotting hulk "Success"

Some escaped convicts became bushrangers, and the north-east area of Victoria was a paradise for their pillaging. The goldfields were thriving, and numerous escort coaches regularly transported the precious metal over dangerously isolated bush tracks.

Many road robbers gained a degree of fame in that era. "Bogong Jack", who in reality was an Omeo butcher named John Payne, achieved notoriety as a successful horse thief. Two of his associates, Thomas Toke and Jack Ahern ("Mitta Mitta Jack"), also gained local acclaim.

The Black Douglas gang mostly plundered travellers between Yackandandah and Castlemaine, before Douglas was captured and hung in Melbourne. Another villain who based himself in Yackandandah was William Turner, better known as "Gypsy" Smith. "Gypsy" was imprisoned for 15 years after being arrested in 1857, and after his release he turned his back on crime and became a successful cattle station manager.

John Fuller Morgan

North-East folklore also recalls the less auspicious exploits of "Billy the Puntman", whose real name was John Hyde. "The Puntman's" career in crime, from the time he started until the time he was captured, allegedly only lasted two hours. This embarrassing performance that earned him the dubious honour of arguably being Australia's least successful bushranger.

Even "the Puntman" had more friends than John Fuller, {commonly known as "Mad Dan" Morgan), a heavy drinker whose unpredictably violent rages caused him to be shunned by fellow bushrangers such as Frank Gardiner and John "Happy Jack" Gilbert.

"Mad Dan" often tortured his victims before murdering them. One of his most vicious crime sprees occurred in Victoria's north-east, where he was finally shot dead at Peechelba Station near Wangaratta after a series of armed robberies, bashings, tortures and arson attacks on local farmers. His passing was widely unlamented.

"Mad Dan" often tortured his victims before murdering them

Ned Kelly

Harry Power, who previously escaped from "Success" in 1865, became the most active bushranger to roam the north-east in the late 1860s. By the time his long criminal career ended, he was a popular figure with many of the general public.

Many admired the impressive way Power defended himself in court appearances, but not Ned Kelly's mother. She sneeringly referred to Power as "the brown paper bushranger". However, in terms of the sheer volume of his crimes, Power's infamous career was more impressive than the legendary Ned. It was Power who first tutored a young Ned Kelly in road robberies around Glenrowan and Myrtleford during the winter of 1869

It was Power who first tutored a young Ned Kelly in road robberies

Power first fell foul of the law in his native Ireland, from where he was transported to Australia for stealing a pair of shoes in August 1840. In the colonies he soon revealed his skills as a horse dealer and thief, and was sentenced to 13 years in gaol after wounding a trooper.

On being released in 1862, Power located himself in Victoria's north-east, but he was soon returned to police custody after again being arrested for stealing horses. Power later made an audacious escape from Melbourne's Pentridge gaol, after hiding himself in a garbage cart that serviced the prison premises. By 1869 he was back in the north-east, where he linked up with the notorious Quinn family at Glenrowan.

Harry Power

Many travellers of that era around Bright, Myrtleford, Mansfield and Longwood were robbed by Power in 1869. During these hold-ups a youthful Ned Kelly often accompanied him.

By November NSW authorities offered a reward of two hundred pounds for information leading to the capture of Power, so he mostly remained in Victoria's north-east where he staged a major hold up at Avenel. During one of his other robberies, Power stole a watch from Robert McBean, a rich and influential squatter, who ensured that the reward for his re-capture was increased.

Finally Power was apprehended in a cold early morning arrest while he was asleep in his bush humpy. At his 1870 trial in Beechworth, Power portrayed himself as a hero to an admiring courtroom audience, but authorities were unimpressed and the "gentleman bushranger" was sentenced to 15 years and six months in custody.

...he drowned in mysterious circumstances in the Murray River

After he was freed in early 1885, the then elderly Power was often accorded celebrity status. He enjoyed providing embellished accounts about his past deeds to various bar room audiences, before he drowned in mysterious circumstances in the Murray River near Swan Hill.

Ned Kelly was hanged five years before Power's final prison term ended, but it was the "gentleman bushranger's" apprentice in crime who became the most famous bushranger of all.

Ned Kelly was born near Beveridge in Victoria around 1855. He was a member of a poor Irish family which lived very much on the fringes of society, and even in his boyhood days he was a "larger than life" character. At the age of 11 Ned saved his drowning neighbour Richard Shelton, and by the time he was a teenager the strongly built lad was in trouble with the law.

In those early formative years, Ned received a three months hard labour sentence for taking delivery of a stolen horse. Initially Ned was charged with stealing the animal, but after it was proved that he was in custody when the theft was committed, a revised charge of receiving a stolen horse was enacted.

Ned's harrowing experiences in prison hardened his outlook against the forces of law and order, especially when he suspected that one of his own horses was stolen by a local constable while he was serving time. Then, in April 1878, Constable Alexander Fitzpatrick allegedly made sexual advances to Ned's sister Kate when he arrived at the family home to arrest Dan Kelly for

Ned's harrowing experiences in prison hardened his outlook against the forces of law...

horse stealing. After Kate's brothers remonstrated strongly with the amorous constable, he charged them all with attempted murder, which further heightened tensions between the police and the Kelly family.

...huge reward of two thousand pounds for the arrest of the Kelly gang.

In late October of that same year, a group of four policemen set out from Mansfield to arrest Ned Kelly, Dan Kelly, Steve Hart and Joe Byrne for horse and cattle stealing.

The mission had tragic results, because when the bushranger gang was cornered at Stringy Bark Creek, a gunfight broke out which resulted in Ned Kelly and Joe Byrne fatally wounding constables Kennedy, Lonigan and Scanlon. Constable McIntyre was the sole survivor, and he managed to return to Mansfield to alert the authorities about the three deaths.

The triple fatalities split community opinion. To the bourgeoisie, and all the forces of law and order and respectability, the three slain troopers were brave men who had been murdered by a gang of dangerous criminals. This section of society applauded the Victorian Government for offering the huge reward of two thousand pounds for the arrest of the Kelly gang.

Conversely, among less affluent members of the community, such as the struggling selectors, the gold fossickers, the descendants of convicts and the Irish poor, legends began to grow about a Robin Hood type prototype. To them Ned Kelly became a hero, a leader who would humble the rich and powerful elements of society and champion the needs of the poor. Ned himself added to this glamorous image. He claimed, after his gang staged bank hold-ups at Euroa and Jerilderie that his men had never harmed a woman, or robbed a poor man.

Joe Byrne shot him dead before fleeing into the night.

These two bank robberies netted the Kelly gang the princely sum of four thousand four hundred pounds. When the authorities mobilised more armed police to hunt them down, the bush-rangers protected themselves with crudely crafted home made armour, fashioned from metal of old farm machinery.

Soon after the Stringy Bark Creek shootings, Aaron Sherritt, who was formerly a close friend of Ned's, was ambushed at his home near Beechworth. Previously Sherritt had been engaged to Joe Byrne's sister, but she ended the relationship when she suspected that he had become a police informer.

On the night of 27th June 1880, Sherritt was entertaining his wife, mother-in-law and four constables at his home, when a knock was heard at the front door. When Sherritt answered the call, Joe Byrne shot him dead before fleeing into the night.

Joe Byrne

Within days Byrne himself perished in the famous siege of Glenrowan, after the gang prepared themselves for a last ditch stand in the town. Telegraph lines were cut down, over 60 locals were held as hostages, and railway workers were forced to rip up the line so that the train transporting police reinforcements from Melbourne would be de-railed.

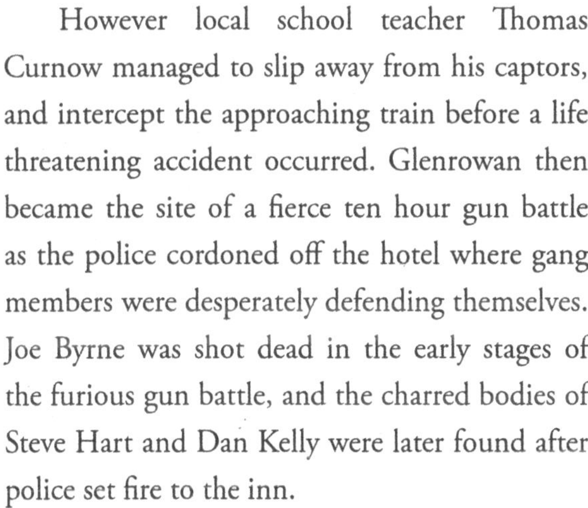

However local school teacher Thomas Curnow managed to slip away from his captors, and intercept the approaching train before a life threatening accident occurred. Glenrowan then became the site of a fierce ten hour gun battle as the police cordoned off the hotel where gang members were desperately defending themselves. Joe Byrne was shot dead in the early stages of the furious gun battle, and the charred bodies of Steve Hart and Dan Kelly were later found after police set fire to the inn.

...railway workers were forced to rip up the line so that the train would be de-railed.

Ned escaped the flame engulfed premises, but reportedly returned to help his comrades after covering his head and torso in home made armour. A hail of bullets aimed at his legs brought him down, however, and the notorious gang leader was taken into custody.

Ned Kelly was charged with the murder of Constable Lonigan, and at his much publicised Melbourne trial, he admitted to the killing but

Over 30,000 people signed a petition opposing Ned Kelly's death sentence...

pleaded self-defence. A bitter verbal exchange occurred between Kelly and Judge Redmond Barry after the defendant was sentenced to death. The bushranger leader informed Barry that "I will see you there (in hell), when you go".

Over 30,000 people signed a petition opposing Ned Kelly's death sentence, but to no avail. He was hung on 11th November 1880, and Ned Kelly's alleged final words were "Such is life."

His memory has lived on through art, literature, books and films, and to this day debate continues about the true significance of Ned Kelly's life. To some, he remains a brutal armed robber and killer. To others, the life of Ned Kelly embraced a growing sense of nationalism, where the shackles of a class ridden English society were rejected, and Australia began to forge a new independent spirit.

CHAPTER TWO:

OFF THE BEATEN TRACK

The first Europeans and Australia's indigenous people clashed from the time white migration first began across the country, with the original squatters annexing the native peoples' land, and the aborigines raiding the stock that the newcomers imported with them.

Some of the early male settlers physically and sexually abused native woman servants on their remote properties. It was this disgraceful practice which resulted in savage reprisals at a Queensland homestead called Hornet Bank in October, 1835.

STUNG INTO ACTION

Originally the property near Hornet Creek was leased by John Fraser, who lived at the homestead with his wife Martha, and their family of five sons and three daughters. After John Fraser died from dysentery, his son, 22-year-old

William "Billy" Fraser, took over the management of the property. This change of ownership was disastrous for female members of the local Jiman aboriginal group, as "Billy" and his brothers sexually assaulted many of the females who were employed by the family.

Tensions escalated rapidly between the two groups, and a revenge attack was planned by a group of male Jimans. One dark October night, just before dawn, about 100 armed aborigines crept towards the homestead where 43-year-old Martha Fraser, her three daughters, four of her sons, and a tutor named John Neagle, were sleeping peacefully.

He also witnessed the female members of his family being raped and bludgeoned to death.

Fourteen-year-old Sylvester "Westy" Fraser was attacked first, and left to die. All other males, including six-year-old James Fraser, were killed by the murderous intruders, while the wounded "Westy" watched from under his camp bed. He also witnessed the female members of his family being raped and bludgeoned to death. The death toll grew to ten, when two white station employees were also killed. After the carnage ended "Westy" staggered 15 kilometres to a neighbouring station to sound the alarm. The teenager survived his gruesome ordeal, and afterwards worked as a carter in the district for many years, though his mental health deteriorated noticeably as the years went by.

Troopers were summoned to the district following the massacre, and two days after the homestead attack occurred, they located an aboriginal group and killed five. More murderous revenge was meted out to other aborigines over the following few months.

...before being either shot or decapitated with sabres.

Unfortunately the Horner Bank massacre was not an isolated event. More carnage took place 200 kilometres north of that property on 17th October 1861. Horatio Spencer Wills, the father of Tom Wills who organised an aboriginal cricket tour of England seven years later, was one of the 19 victims.

The death toll continued to grow in various feuds between the ethnic groups. By 1866 a total of 600 whites and 5,000-15,000 blacks had been murdered, and in Queensland the carnage of aboriginal people rose to an alarming 30,000 by 1894.

Race based murders were not only confined to the northern state. In June 1838 at Myall Creek, in the north-west of NSW, about 30 aboriginal women and children were roped together by a group of Europeans. They were then either shot or decapitated with sabres.

A large funeral pyre removed much of the evidence, but to the surprise of many the culprits were hunted down and punished. Seven men were charged and later hung after being found guilty of murder, which produced angry reactions from many disbelieving local whites.

A memorial stone was put in place at the Myall Creek site in 2001, and a ceremony noting this historic event is now conducted annually.

OUTRAGE IN CEDUNA

Rupert Maxwell Stuart was an illiterate part-aboriginal raised by the Aranda tribe. He became a stockman by the age of ten, and spent the next seventeen years labouring in the outback, and earning money in the boxing ring at various agricultural shows. His sister taught him to laboriously write his own name in block letters, which was his only literate skill.

Stuart was particularly attracted by one of the women...

In December 1958, 27-year-old "Maxie" Stuart was employed as a labourer with Gieseman's Funland Carnival, which arrived in the South Australian outback town of Ceduna six days before Christmas.

That evening Stuart and a carnival companion attended the local picture theatre, and when the movie ended the drunken duo pestered a group of young local women, who caught a taxi to avoid their unwanted attentions. Stuart was particularly attracted by one of the women, and next day he tried in vain to locate her in Ceduna.

Rupert Stuart

The frustrated man once more turned to alcohol for solace, and early that afternoon it was a resentful Max Stuart who lurched towards the beach on his way back to work at Funland.

...black trackers declared that the nearby footprints were left by an Aranda person...

Late that afternoon, nine-year-old Mary Olive Hattam was reported missing from the beach near Ceduna. Close to midnight, her badly battered and sexually molested body was found in a cave near where she had been playing. Police also found a large blood stained rock, which the murderer had used to fracture the child's skull. After arriving later at the death scene, black trackers declared that the nearby footprints were left by an Aranda person, and that the trail led back to the Ceduna road.

Since 9.30 that evening Stuart had been placed in custody for drunken behaviour. After spending the night in gaol, he missed linking up again with the carnival group before they moved out of town on 21st December. Stuart's freedom was short-lived, as he was arrested after black-trackers were either persuaded, or became convinced, that his footprints were identical to those found at the murder scene. After intense and perhaps violent interrogation from six policemen, Stuart signed a written confession to the murder with his customary block letter signature.

At his first trial on December 20th 1959,

...he was convinced that the words written in the confession were not uttered by an illiterate outback aboriginal.

Stuart denied the crime, and claimed in his short verbal defence that police physically harassed him into signing his "confession". Proceedings took a surprising turn, when the coroner assigned to the case, changed her previous time decision of when the murder occurred. Stuart, however, was still found guilty as charged and sentenced to death.

When an application for appeal was denied, opinions about the process followed in the Stuart case began to divide Australians. The police remained adamant that the written confession was recorded in Stuart's own words, but Father Thomas Dixon publicly expressed his scepticism about this claim.

Dixon discussed the case with Stuart in the Aranda language, and he was convinced that the words written in the confession were not uttered by an illiterate outback aboriginal. After a second appeal application failed, and the Privy Council in London rejected another bid for a re-trial, it seemed the death sentence on Stuart would be enacted.

Fortunately crucial new evidence then emerged. The Giesman Funland carnival group were located near Mt Isa in North Queensland, and three employees confirmed that Stuart was working with or near them at the carnival, when the murder took place between 2–4 pm. The Adelaide print media had long been critical about the conduct of the case, and many in the public also called for a reinvestigation of the crime, the state premier, Sir Thomas Playford, established a Royal Commission to fully investigate the evidence.

Cynics noted however that two of the three appointed commissioners had sat in previous review team which had rejected other appeals for Stuart, and the Adelaide press declared that any findings would be a farce. Stuart's legal spokesman resigned in disgust, but nearly 40 days after the 11 week hearing began, the man who had been on "death row" a harrowing seven times during the long drawn out proceedings, had his sentence reduced to life imprisonment.

...the man who had been on "death row" a harrowing seven times...

Rupert Maxwell Stuart, a half-caste who had been rejected all his life by two widely different Australian cultures, was finally released from gaol after serving 14 years.

Until 1984 he continued to serve gaol terms for minor offences, before he was released for the sixth and final time from Yatala Prison.

By then in custody he had learned to speak proper English, he had become literate, he was a water colour painter, and had acquired work skills.

Stuart married after being finally released and settled at Santa Theresa Mission near Alice Springs. He became an Aranda elder, and served as Chairman of the Central Land Council during the late 1990's.

RACIAL TENSION IN RURAL NSW

...threatened to kill another indigenous youth with a machete...

By the 1990s, the NSW outback town of Walgett was a depressing example of a racially torn and socially deprived society. Unemployment benefits were the principal source of income, and alcohol and other abuse substance were rife, especially in the large aboriginal section of the community. Brendan and Vester Fernando were two indigenous locals who regularly attracted the attention of local police.

Twenty-three-year-old Brendan Fernando had been a heavy user of marijuana and heroin since the age of ten, and it was suspected that regular sniffing of petrol had caused him permanent brain damage. This dangerous habit may have contributed to his exceedingly low IQ reading of 60, and he was habitually "spaced out" on drugs, alcohol and medication. Twenty-four-year-old Vester Fernando had been an alcoholic since he was 16, and both cousins had served several jail terms for violent offences.

By late evening on Thursday 8th December, the Fernando cousins were dangerously out of control. Around 11.30 pm Vester threatened to kill another indigenous youth with a machete. The pair then lurched to the local hospital car park where they attempted to steal a vehicle.

Sandra Hoare, who was engaged to a policeman stationed in the town, and had just begun a nursing career in Walgett, was spotted by the duo near a window inside one of the wards. They immediately feared that their stealing attempt had been spotted. Consequently they burst into the hospital premises, bashed an elderly patient, and abducted the young nurse after threatening her with their long handled machete.

...he then virtually decapitated her with the machete.

The unfortunate woman was then marched through the darkness to a nearby oval, where she was bashed and stripped. Brendan held Sandra Hoare's legs apart while Vester sexually assaulted her, and he then virtually decapitated her with the machete.

The next day a massive search began for the abducted woman, and her mutilated body was found that afternoon. The battered hospital patient had described the assailants to police, and several aboriginal camps and houses were raided at gunpoint, as the situation in town grew increasingly tense.

Fortunately police soon gained the vital information they needed. The aboriginal who had been threatened earlier that evening implicated the Fernandos, and Brendan was soon arrested. Two days later Vester was located 300 kilometres away at his sister's home in Dubbo.

Cassette tapes from the stolen car were found in his possession, and the Fernando cousins were charged with murder.

On 21st August 1997, both were sentenced to life imprisonment, with the added recommendation from Justice Abadee that they never be released. The violent young offenders were the first indigenous people to receive such a harsh sentence.

Two years later Vester stabbed his cousin to death in Lithgow Prison, and he is now confined in the High Risk Management Unit at Goulburn goal. Where he has become a devout Muslim.

QUESTIONS REMAIN IN OUTBACK MYSTERY

Bradley Murdoch received a life sentence in July 2004 for the murder of Peter Falconio, but issues continue to surface in this mystifying case.

It was a controversial situation from the time the 28-year-old Englishman disappeared in Australia's vast and lonely outback on the evening of July 14th 2001. His body has never been found, no murder weapon was discovered, and no known motive for the murder was established.

His body has never been found...

All available evidence appeared to be circumstantial, until Falconio's 27-year-old girlfriend

Bradley Murdoch

Joanne Lees had her stained T-shirt and the steering wheel of the couples' Kombi van, analysed by forensic experts. The DNA uncovered supposedly matched that of the accused man. It was probably this vital evidence which convinced the Darwin jury that Bradley John Murdoch was guilty of the murder of Peter Falconio, as well as the assault and abduction of Joanne Lees.

A sensational new twist was added to this forensic evidence however in December 2007, when the same DNA test that resulted in the conviction of Murdoch, was ruled inadmissible by a British court because of its unreliability. Murdoch has lodged two appeals against his conviction — neither has been successful. The High Court of Australia refused special leave to appeal his conviction on 21 June 2007, leaving Murdoch with no further avenues of appeal.

...a fast moving vehicle suddenly loomed up behind them...

Falconio and his English girlfriend came to Australia for an extended holiday in the year 2001. They spent some time in Sydney, before purchasing a second hand orange Kombi van to travel to more remote parts of the country, and around 4 pm on 14th July the pair departed from Alice Springs. After sharing a joint of cannabis while they watched an outback sunset near the Ti Tree roadhouse, they continued their journey up the lonely Stuart Highway.

"Are you going to rape me? Have you shot my boyfriend?"

Lees later recalled that she felt nervous about their isolation, and persuaded her lover not to stop and extinguish a few small spot fires that were burning near the roadside. Then, around 7.30–8 pm, it is alleged that a fast moving vehicle suddenly loomed up behind them. As it drew alongside, the driver gestured urgently towards the back of their Kombi van. Despite dim visibility, Lees later provided a detailed description of the man's appearance, and she was also able to describe the dog that sat next to him in the driver's cabin.

Falconio was concerned that sparks might be flying out of the rear of the old van, and he ignored Lees' misgivings and pulled to a halt. When he joined the stranger at the back of the vehicle, he asked Lees to press her foot on the accelerator a few times. Following this request, Lees presumed that the old van was back-firing when she heard a couple of small explosions. However, the apparently mundane situation changed abruptly, when a stranger appeared at the driver's window and pointed a silver revolver menacingly at her head.

The man tied Lees' hands behind her with some home made handcuffs, and threw the struggling young woman next to the docile dog in his own vehicle. As he drew a canvas bag over her, she cried in anguish "Are you going to rape me? Have you shot my boyfriend?"

"No", was the curt answer from the assailant, whom she later described a man of medium build with a black cap. She dislodged the bag from her head while she lay on the back of the white utility tray, and Joanne Lees then heard the ominous sound of something being dragged along the gravel on the side of the road.

After pushing herself off the tray she fell heavily on the road, but the still handcuffed woman managed to dash into the low scrub where she hid under a small bush. The cursing stranger seized a torch from his vehicle, and looked for her in the darkness. Then, after abandoning his brief search, he drove the Kombi van a short distance from the crime scene, and departed in his own vehicle

The terrified young woman remained in hiding for a considerable time, not trusting the sound of the few other sedans that passed by in case it was her returning assailant. Hours later however, she heard the unmistakable and welcome sound of a heavy road train approaching, and the still handcuffed Joanne Lees ran to the side of the road, and waved her arms frantically to attract the driver's attention.

...there was a man somewhere in the darkness who had shot her boyfriend...

Vince Miller was at the wheel of the truck, and the startled man quickly applied the brakes when he saw her, and finally brought the huge vehicle to a halt about a kilometre further on.

Falconio & Lees

He feared that he had run over the woman, and anxiously searched for a body after jumping out of the driver's cabin. To his relief, Lees soon emerged from under the now stationary truck crying for help. Miller and his co-driver Rodney Brown then cut her handcuffs free, and attempted to calm the now hysterical victim.

However when she screamed that there was a man somewhere in the darkness who had shot her boyfriend, the pair rejected any thought of searching for the missing Falconio, and they drove the traumatised woman back to safe refuge at the Barrow Creek Hotel. There the Alice Springs police were contacted, and an investigating team arrived approximately three hours later.

Was it possible that Peter Falconio was still alive?

Frictions arose almost immediately between Lees, the Northern Territory (NT) police and the media. Lees appeared to find the type of questions asked by both groups to be irritating and intrusive, and she was reluctant to co-operate with police and media interviews. They in turn found her constant complaints about their inability to find Peter, her need for personal privacy, and her initial refusal to communicate with her parents, to be disturbing behaviour. In this atmosphere of mutual distrust, many unanswered questions surfaced.

Why were there so many discrepancies emerging in Joanne Lees' evidence? What was the motive for the killing or abduction? Was it possible that Peter Falconio was still alive? If he was deceased, where was his body? How did she manage to evade her torch carrying attacker in such low scrub? Why didn't he use his dog to help locate her? Why was she only superficially injured after allegedly being thrown onto the roadside and punched around the head? Why was there no sign of splatter blood that usually resulted from a close range shot?

...two credible eye witnesses claimed that they saw Peter Falconio eight days after his alleged disappearance.

While Lees and Falconio lived in Sydney, she had a brief affair with an English backpacker, which raised doubts about the true strength of their relationship. Observers also wondered if the assailant and the English couple had either met or seen each other before that fateful night. It was also curious that Lee described her attacker as being of "average height", when Murdoch was later revealed as being a very tall, strongly built man. Public interest in the case became even more intense, when two credible eye witnesses claimed that they saw Peter Falconio eight days after his alleged disappearance.

Teacher aide Robert Brown and his partner Melissa Kendall, who later became an assistant registrar in their home town of Bourke, both swear that on 22nd July they observed Falconio with three other adults at a Bourke petrol station.

...he could permanently dispose of a body with ease in the outback.

The group supposedly drove away in a dark green utility, but unfortunately police were not notified about the reported sighting until the next day. By then the alleged group had vanished into the vast remote areas of the Australian outback, and no trace of them has currently surfaced. Near that time there were also less convincing reports that Falconio had been spotted as far apart as Mt. Isa and Terrigal.

An identikit photograph of a long haired suspect with a droopy moustache was compiled from Lees' recollections and widely circulated, but received no worthwhile public response. Finally police investigations received a boost on 16th May 2002, after James Hepi was arrested near his South Australian property with 3.5 kilograms of cannabis in his vehicle. Hepi was convinced that his co-drug runner Bradley James Murdoch had "dobbed" on him to the police. In the hope of receiving a more lenient sentence, he provided information about the Broome resident's supposed link with Peter Falconio's disappearance.

Murdoch allegedly boasted to Hepi that he could permanently dispose of a body with ease in the outback. Furthermore, since returning to his home base, Murdoch had greatly altered his own appearance, as well as the design of his white utility. Interest in the new suspect increased when it was revealed that Murdoch was previously gaoled for 21 months in May 1995, after firing several shots at a group of aborigines he had argued with at Fitzroy Crossing. The dangerous altercation was fortunately free of casualties, and Murdoch surrendered voluntarily to the police shortly afterwards.

On 28th August 2002, an armed Murdoch was arrested by police at gunpoint outside a Port Augusta supermarket. Blood samples were taken from the suspect, and by 10th October it was declared that Murdoch's DNA matched the sample derived from blood stains found on Joanne Lees' shirt, and the steering wheel of the Kombi van.

Murdoch answered multiple charges of abduction and rape...

The much awaited murder trial was delayed, however, while Murdoch answered multiple charges of abduction and rape against a woman and her 12-year-old daughter in South Australia. He was ultimately cleared of all charges in this case, but was apprehended by police immediately after the state court reached its decision, and transferred to the Darwin remand centre, from where he faced future committal proceedings in the Falconio case.

The trial began on May 17th 2004. Joanne Lees appeared as a crown witness, and Peter Falconio's family also travelled from England for the much publicised event.

Murdoch pleaded not guilty. He denied that he handcuffed Lees, and could not explain how his DNA apparently matched the incriminating stains. His defence barrister attempted to cast doubts about the credibility of Hepi and Lees as witnesses. It was also intimated that the police had tampered with evidence to gain the DNA result that suited their investigations.

...could not explain how his DNA apparently matched the incriminating stains.

The evidence of 85 witnesses was heard, and 350 exhibits viewed in this exhaustive eight week trial, but finally the jury found Bradley John Murdoch guilty of all charges and he received a life sentence of 28 years.

Murdoch continues to maintain his innocence, and in February 2007 an appeal process began in an attempt to quash the murder conviction. These attempts seemingly came to an end in June of that year, after the Australian High Court rejected his last opportunity of appeal, but since then other issues arising from the case have come to public attention.

On December 8th 2007 the "Melbourne Age" reported that Murdoch was attempting to use the conduct of the NT Chief Magistrate's daughter as a trigger to have his case re-examined.

Joanne Martin, the daughter of Chief Magistrate Brian Martin, gave birth to a baby whose father had links with Murdoch's Darwin court case. This attempt by Murdoch to show a conflict of interest appeared to lack credibility, when the Chief Magistrate claimed that there was nothing legally improper in the relationship. The couple, he asserted, did not meet until well after Murdoch's trial. The NT Legal Aid Commission, which initiated investigations on behalf of Murdoch, agreed with this opinion which effectively ended Murdoch's hopes.

"How can I tell them where the body is when I don't know?"

Previously, when Murdoch sought a gaol transfer from Darwin to be near his aging mother in Western Australia, the NT police offered to accommodate his wishes if he revealed the whereabouts of Falconio's body. Murdoch responded to this ultimatum by saying "How can I tell them where the body is when I don't know?"

The twists and turns of this mystifying case continues to fascinate the Australian public.

CHAPTER THREE:

OUT OF CONTROL

FIRST WOMAN HUNG IN THE WEST

After 60-year-old John Hurford prospered from his farming, whaling and timber ventures in Western Australia, he married a widow 30 years his junior. The union between he and his wife Bridget was not a happy one, and by April 1855 Hurford moved away from the marital home to a neighbour's house.

Overcrowding there caused him to return to his own residence, but about a month later he became ill, and passed away in the night. At the inquest which followed, little notice was taken of bruise marks around his neck and stomach regions.

Soon after her husband's death, Bridget openly became involved in a sexual relationship with ex-convict Enoch Dodd, who John Hurford had previously hired to work on his property. In a moment of drunken candour, Dodd informed a friend that he battered and strangled John Hurford in his bed, for which Bridget rewarded him with one hundred pounds, and her late husband's horse

Word of his confession reached Governor Kennedy, who had the pair arrested. Despite largely circumstantial evidence, Enoch Dodd and Bridget Hurford were found guilty of murder and sentenced to death. She believed the forces of law and order would not hang a woman, but her gender failed to save her from the gallows.

...the first woman to be legally hung...

On October 15th 1855, Bridget Hurford became the first woman to be legally hung in Western Australia.

A FATAL CHANGE OF MIND

Justice Clancy made it abundantly clear that he believed the death penalty he imposed on Len Lawson should take place, after the Sydney artist raped two of the five models he abducted in 1954. However not only was the death sentence commuted to life imprisonment; Lawson walked free in the latter months of 1960, after a NSW Labor Government reduced his maximum sentence to 14 years. This lenient attitude later proved to be a fatal mistake.

Len Lawson was raised in a loving middle class family, and topped his Intermediate class at Wagga Wagga High School. The popular and handsome 15-year-old then began work as an apprentice commercial artist in Sydney, before embarking on a freelance career two years later. The future appeared bright when Lawson became the illustrator of the "Lone Avenger" and "Hooded Rider" comic book characters, but a dark side to his talents began to emerge. Lawson began selling pornographic pictures, and some of the women he sketched appeared to be dead.

"Lone Avenger" comic

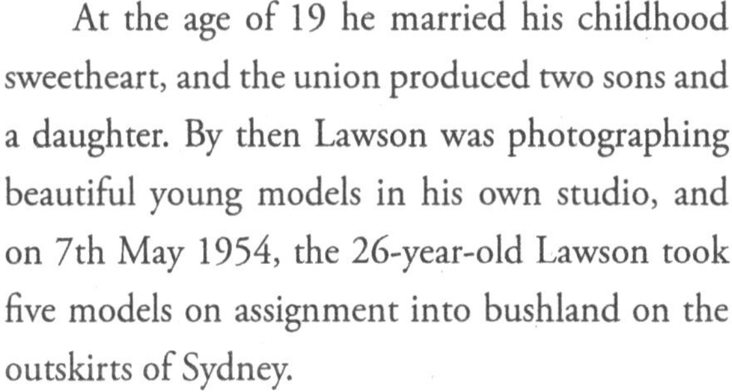

At the age of 19 he married his childhood sweetheart, and the union produced two sons and a daughter. By then Lawson was photographing beautiful young models in his own studio, and on 7th May 1954, the 26-year-old Lawson took five models on assignment into bushland on the outskirts of Sydney.

Once there he produced a .22 rifle and a hunting knife, and tied rope around the wrists and ankles of the terrified young women. All his victims were molested when he cut off their clothing, and when they were naked he gagged them with sticking plaster.

...when they were naked he gagged them with sticking plaster.

After parading naked in front of his hostages, Lawson raped a 19-year-old model in front of her colleagues, before forcing a 22-year-old married victim to also have sex with him. Later an apparently remorseful Lawson threatened to commit suicide, but relented when he was told that nothing would be divulged. Predictably this agreement was broken, and the police were waiting for Lawson when he returned to his studio.

...the women were willing partners to group sex...

Lawson claimed that the women were willing partners to group sex after his trial began on 24th June 1954, but was found guilty by the jury. Experts declared that Lawson was a psychopath, but in gaol he was a model prisoner. He became a devout Catholic, and the biblical paintings that Lawson produced on the walls of the Goulburn Prison chapel were much admired. His portraits were even considered worthy of entry in the prestigious Archibald Prize Exhibition, before it was realised that the works were ineligible, because his art was created from photographs instead of live models.

The "reformed" man gained his release from a minimum security prison late in 1960, and he then lived with his parents in Moss Vale. Lawson's wife had left him during that time in custody, and he showed no inclination to see his children again.

By August 1961, Len Lawson moved to the fashionable Sydney suburb of Collaroy, and resumed his career as a commercial artist. In this role, he met and befriended Jane Bower and her mother, and the trio regularly went on outings together. Five weeks after they met, Lawson took Jane Bower back to his home, where he supposedly intended to continue her portrait.

There he made advances on her, and when she resisted Lawson struck Jane Bowers on the head with a sand filled sock and tied the unconscious girl's wrists together before having intercourse with her. When she regained consciousness, Jane was first strangled before a hunting knife was plunged into her chest. Lawson then slid the dead girl's pants back over her buttocks, and wrote in eyebrow pencil on her stomach "God forgive me, Len".

After writing a confessional letter to his parents, Lawson drove 200 kilometres south to Moss Vale. After sleeping overnight in his car, he arrived at the local Church of England Grammar School as the lessons for the day began. When students and teachers arrived at the school chapel for Morning Prayer, Lawson stopped them at gunpoint and threatened to tie them up and use them as hostages.

...a hunting knife was plunged into her chest.

The police had meanwhile been called, and when a distracted Lawson watched a group of officers arrive, the Headmistress, Ms. Jean Turnbull, attempted to wrestle Lawson's rifle from him. Five shots rang out during the struggle, and 15-year-old student Wendy Luscombe unfortunately received a fatal wound.

At his second trial a jury only took 17 minutes to find him guilty of two murders, and he received a life imprisonment sentence. How-

...he grabbed a performing artist around the neck at a gaol concert...

ever the predatory Lawson remained a danger in prison. In 1972 he grabbed a performing artist around the neck at a gaol concert, and held a knife at her throat while he ordered everyone from the room. Fortunately he was subdued after other inmates struggled with him, but Ms. Sharon Hamilton, the target of Lawson's attack, required surgery for the knife wounds she received in the attack.

In June of that year, Len Lawson, who had been the secretary of the gaol arts and craft group which organised the visiting concert, received an additional five years on his life sentence after pleading guilty to a malicious wounding charge. He was transferred to the maximum security section of Grafton Gaol to serve the remainder of his sentence.

On November 29th 2003 Len Lawson died after serving 48 years in custody. Several paintings created by this violent man currently hang in the prison where he died.

GUILTY OF ADULTERY AND MURDER?

Leith McDonald Ratten was 21 when he married in 1960, and four years later he moved with his wife Beverly to Echuca, where he became a successful surveyor. The young couple were regular church goers, and soon became friendly with their neighbours Peter and Jenny Kemp, with the two husbands sharing a common love of shooting and fishing trips.

Shortly after both couples celebrated the births of a third child, Peter Kemp began a new occupation as a sports goods salesman, and the Ratten's close friends moved to nearby Barham. Peter's new job often took him away from home, and Leith Ratten formed the habit of dropping in to see the lonely Jenny when he was shooting in the Barham area. By April 1969 they began an affair, despite the fact that Beverly Ratten was pregnant again.

...habit of dropping in to see the lonely Jenny...

The adulterous husband soon appeared to have misgivings about his new involvement, as he applied for various positions in a 1970 Antarctic expedition, which required a 12 month commitment from him far from home. He and Jenny Kemp allegedly discussed divorce arrangements from their respective spouses, and they met with a Shepparton solicitor in May 1970.

At that time Jenny Kemp discussed a divorce settlement with her husband, and believed that Ratten had initiated similar discussions with his wife, though she understood that there would be no firm decisions made until the Ratten's fourth child had been born. Beverly Ratten gave no indication to friends or family that she knew anything about the affair, and Leith Ratten later claimed that he never divulged that information to his wife, and that he never intended to leave her.

Both she and the unborn baby were dead...

On 7th May 1970, Leith Ratten was cleaning rust from a gun in his kitchen. Beverly was also present, and Echuca telephonist Janet Flowers later recalled a high pitched female type voice urgently requesting a police presence at 59 Mitchell Street. A sobbing four-year-old Wendy Ratten was outside the house when police arrived, and when her father ushered them inside, the body of Beverly Ratten lay on the floor next to a shotgun. Both she and the unborn baby were dead, and the distressed husband claimed that the gun misfired accidentally while she was making a cup of coffee.

Jenny Kemp assured police that Leith Ratten was incapable of murdering his wife when she informed police about their affair, but the homicide squad was soon investigating the case. Under intense questioning, Ratten maintained his account about the gun discharging accidentally, even though his assertion seemed at odds with the point of entry of the bullet. He also asserted that Beverly would have agreed to a divorce if that was his wish, which contradicted Jenny Kemp's alleged understanding of the situation.

She was led to believe that Beverly would never countenance divorce proceedings being implemented, because of her strong religious beliefs. Ratten informed police that he never had any intention of leaving his wife, and that Beverly had not phoned the telephone exchange on the day that she died. After concluding their investigations, police charged Leith Ratten with the murder of his wife and his court case began in Shepparton on 10th August 1970.

At the trial much was made of Ratten's deceit to his wife and mistress. Even though there were no witnesses to the shooting, and the bulk of evidence against him was circumstantial in nature, Ratten was found guilty of murder on 20th August, and sentenced to 25 years imprisonment.

Beverly had not phoned the telephone exchange on the day that she died.

In 1974 the High Court rejected an appeal against the Supreme Court decision, despite strong support from writer-lawyer Tom Molomby, who comprehensively examined the case in his book "Ratten: The Web of Circumstance". New state premier John Cain ordered a re-examination of the case in April 1982, but within a month this new attempt had failed to provide any compelling new evidence.

Leith McDonald Ratten finally served out his full sentence in a minimum security gaol before being released, and he then moved to

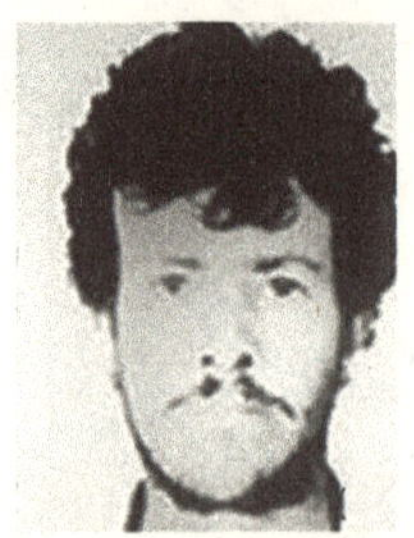
Allan Baker

Kevin Crump

Queensland to work as a surveyor.

A DISGUSTING DUO

In 1972 two decidedly evil people became friends after Kevin Gary Crump and Allan Baker met in gaol, and their unsavoury relationship finally resulted in two innocent people being brutally murdered.

After being released from custody, Baker was employed for three weeks as a farm labourer with the Morse family near Collarenebri, and he was well treated by his employers. By early November he and Crump re-united, and they shot dead Ian James Lamb near Narrabri. Robbery was the main motive for the unprovoked attack on the young cotton picker, but the dangerous pair only netted $20 from the robbery.

Crump and Baker emerged from hiding and abducted his wife at gunpoint.

They then returned to the Morse family's Banaway Station, and after Brian Morse drove away in the early morning, Crump and Baker emerged from hiding and abducted his wife at gunpoint. Virginia Morse, a mother of three, was forced to accompany them 190 kilometres to their camp site. There she was staked to the ground, raped, shot dead and molested again, before being thrown into a nearby river.

On 13th November 1973, a policeman was

wounded in the head when shots were exchanged after the pair raided a house at Cessnock. Shortly afterwards Crump and Baker were captured at Woodville in the Hunter Valley, when their car became bogged during a police chase.

After Crump made a full confession on 20th July 1974, the pair faced trial and many in the court room were appalled when the accused often sniggered and leered to each other during their trial, when evidence was presented about their brutal crimes. In custody, while serving life imprisonment sentences, the pair was separated after they became a homosexual couple.

...the accused often snig-gered and leered to each other during their trial...

Crump was denied gaol release in 2003, while Baker's lawyers requested that his sentence be reduced to a minimum of 30 years.

THE LONELY HEARTS KILLER

"Not fit to be in society" and "sentenced for the term of your natural life". These were damning conclusions reached about Rodney Francis Cameron after he was found guilty of the 1974 murders of a man and a woman. However, despite the apparent finality of his sentence, Cameron was freed after 16 years in gaol, a decision which effectively renewed his license to kill.

...police discovered a towel stuffed down her throat...

Cameron was adopted before he turned seven after both his parents died, and from his early childhood years he was constantly in trouble for his vicious attacks on females. At the age of ten he tried to strangle a girl, and his dangerous behaviour caused his adoptive parents to reject him by the time he reached adolescent years.

In 1974 Rodney Cameron became a trainee nurse, and on 31st January he raped and murdered 49-year-old nurse Florence Jackson. She had befriended the teenager at the Katoomba nursing home where they both worked, and police discovered a towel stuffed down her throat when they arrived at the Blue Mountains murder scene.

Cameron was then on the run, and a week later, when he was hitchhiking towards Victoria, he murdered 19-year-old bank clerk Francesco Gilberto, who had kindly provided Cameron with transport. Gilberto was bashed with a boulder before being strangled with a football sock. Cameron again left his distinguishing "calling card": the victim's shirt was stuffed down his throat.

The fugitive continued his violent behaviour when he headed north towards Queensland. He threatened to kill a mother and her daughter whom he had abducted, before he was arrested on 21st February 1974. Cameron was sentenced to nine years by a NSW court and "for the term of his natural life" in Victoria.

However, in an act which caused at least one more death, and possibly as many as five, Cameron was released back into society on 12th March 1990, after successfully appealing his sentence. Previously, in 1986, he had married his life long companion Anne while still serving his sentence, and it was believed that his life had been rehabilitated. Cameron made a promising start in his return to mainstream life, gaining a position as manager of a Sunbury stud farm.

It did not take long for the dark side of his personality to re-emerge. On 26th May 1990, Cameron arranged a meeting with Melbourne woman Maria Goeliner who he initially made contact with on a 3AW radio match making program. The pair decided to rendezvous at Katoomba, where they booked in at the Rider Motor Inn.

Several hours later Goeliner was discovered dead in their motel unit. She had been bashed and strangled, a handkerchief had been shoved down her throat, and a bunch of yellow carnations was placed on her body. A note had also been left which in part read "Anne, I am sorry. Had I not done what happened, my life would have been destroyed. Love eternally, Rodney."

...claiming that a mysterious third person had murdered the unfortunate woman...

A week later, at Deniliquin near the NSW/

Victorian border, Cameron voluntarily surrendered to local police, claiming that a mysterious third person named Frederick Mulner had murdered the unfortunate woman in Katoomba. Police found him to be quiet and polite, but completely lacking in compassion. "The most dangerous man you would probably ever meet," was the assessment of one of the investigating officers.

Rodney Francis Cameron, who was dubbed "the lonely hearts killer" by the tabloid press of the day, was found guilty of murder once more, and received a life imprisonment sentence with the recommendation that he "never be released".

More horrific murders have since been attributed to Cameron. Five months after he was charged with the "lonely hearts" homicide, he was named as the murderer of Sydney pensioner Sarah McKenzie. This killing occurred nearly 20 years previously, but three days before the 1994 trial began the case was nobbled because of a lack of conclusive evidence.

...dubious honour of being Australia's most prolific serial killer.

However on 3rd October 1997, the then 42-year-old Cameron admitted his guilt in that murder case. He later confessed to a series of other killings; two Melbourne murders in 1990, and two more 1974 slayings – one in South Australia, and the other in NSW.

"I know that I'll rot in jail, but I want to

clean the slate," he confided to a friend.

If the claims of Rodney Francis Cameron are true, this chilling murderer claimed eight victims, which would gain him the dubious honour of being Australia's most prolific serial killer.

THE BEWILDERING MEGAN KALAJZICH CASE

On 27th January 1986, Megan Kalajzich was found in her Manly home in Sydney with two fatal shot wounds in her left cheek. Two bullets were also retrieved from her husband's pillow, and Andrew Kalajzich later described the gunman as being a tall man, of foreign appearance, who was approximately in his mid 40s.

Two bullets were also retrieved from her husband's pillow...

Police soon ascertained that no forced entry had been made into the couples' bedroom, and tended to believe that the killer had accessed the building via the upstairs balcony. The murder followed a report that Megan Kalajzich had been assaulted at home by a man wearing a balaclava, 16 days before her death,

That incident was preceded by a previous scare for Mrs Kalajzich in September 1973, when her son Andrew Kalajzich junior and she escaped unscathed from a car crash. On that occasion her husband was driving the vehicle, but he fortuitously jumped to safety just before the car crashed into an embankment. He later claimed that he blacked out while at the wheel, but instinctively jumped to safety when he regained consciousness, and saw the embankment suddenly loom up.

Kalajzich senior originally emigrated from Yugoslavia to Sydney, where he acquired much wealth with his food retail outlets and property development interests. In one of his fish and chip shops he employed an attractive young woman called Lydia, with whom he ultimately shared a volatile extra-marital relationship.

He reneged on the arrangement, however, after he saw his intended victim..

On more than one alleged occasion, Kalajzich convinced Lydia that they were free to marry, but the anticipated wedding ceremonies were regularly cancelled at short notice. He was also rumoured to be courting Marlene Watson, who was his secretary.

During this time of real and rumoured relationships, Andrew Kalajzich senior reportedly asked his security officer, Warren Elkins, to locate a "hit man" to target his wife Megan. At first "black George" Canellis was recruited for a fee of $25,000. He reneged on the arrangement, however, after he saw his intended victim, though he only returned $20,000 of his original payment. Finally Bill Vandenberg, the man who donned a balaclava in the botched murder attempt on Mrs. Kalajzich on January 11th, agreed to attempt the murder once more.

...her relationship with him had cooled after being repeatedly "stood up"...

Vandenberg faced various unforseen hurdles in his killing quest. A locked back door to the apartment foiled at least five attempts, before he finally shot Megan Kalajzich at close range in the main bedroom. After her husband rolled off the bed onto the floor, the gunman then fired two more bullets into the pillow next to the murder victim. Andrew Kalajzich senior then escorted Vandenberg from the building and locked the back door behind him.

Canellis then decided to clear his name in this murder case, and after he was "wired" in conversations with Vandenberg, Warren Elkins also came under suspicion. After his flat was raided by police, Vandenberg admitted his guilt, and on the 15th February 1986, he, his friend Henry Orrock, Elkins and Kalajzich senior, were all taken into custody.

Watson firmly denied she had had any sexual or romantic involvement with Andrew Kalajzich senior, and Lydia claimed her relationship with him had cooled after being repeatedly "stood up". The charges against the wealthy tycoon were therefore dismissed because of the lack of a clear motive.

However Kalajzich attempted to bribe Van-

...the remorseful man hung himself in his gaol cell.

denberg into making the false claim that he, (Andrew Kalajzich senior), was not involved in the killing. This move became counter productive after a frightened Vandenberg strongly implicated Kalajzich's involvement, and the wealthy businessman was re-arrested.

When sentences were handed down in court, Vandenberg, Orrock and Kalajzich received life terms, while Elkins was given a ten-year term for conspiring to murder Megan Kalajzich. Vandenberg blamed himself for the harsh sentence Orrocks received, and the remorseful man hung himself in his gaol cell.

Andrew Kalajzich's appeal was rejected, but he became obsessed with gaining freedom, spending as much as $100,000 a week on legal fees, before his money evaporated, in unsuccessful attempts to clear his name. Kalajzich survived a Lithgow Prison knife attack in April 1993.

During his many years in gaol, he has been frequently visited by Marlene Watson, his mother, his mother-in-law and popular radio host Alan Jones, who have all supported Kalajzich's consistent claims of innocence in this bungled and contradictory case, but another appeal was rejected in 1998.

THE MUTILATION OF ANITA COBBY

Anita Cobby

Over 30 years ago, the pack rape and murder of a popular and beautiful young woman by five strangers shocked the nation.

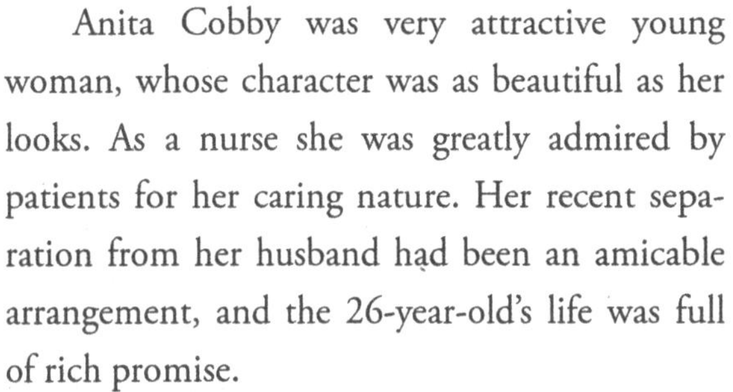

Anita Cobby was very attractive young woman, whose character was as beautiful as her looks. As a nurse she was greatly admired by patients for her caring nature. Her recent separation from her husband had been an amicable arrangement, and the 26-year-old's life was full of rich promise.

Optimistic expectations ended abruptly on 2nd February 1986. The early hours of that hot Sydney summer evening had been enjoyed by Anita with nursing friends at a city restaurant. Later she was strolling to her parents' home from the Blacktown railway station around 8.45 pm, when the occupants of a stolen Holden sedan randomly selected her as a victim for their sexual fantasies.

...the occupants of a stolen Holden sedan randomly selected her as a victim for their sexual fantasies.

After the car screeched to a stop beside her, Anita was dragged inside by two males before the vehicle sped away. Next day, on the outskirts of the suburb, the naked body of the innocent young woman was discovered in a paddock by a farmer. Anita Cobby had been grossly sexually assaulted, before her head was nearly severed from her neck

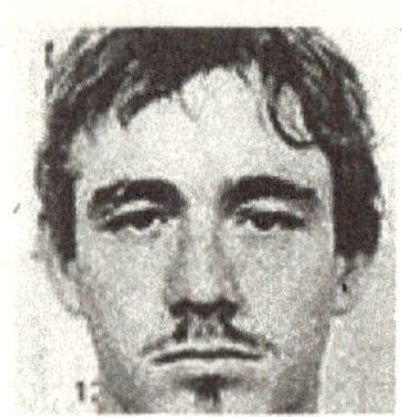
Les Murphy

by a deep knife wound.

Neville Wran, the then NSW premier who previously met Anita when she was an entrant in a beauty contest, immediately offered a reward of $50,000 for information that would lead to convictions for those responsible for this horrific crime.

By 17th February, police received information that linked 20-year-old John Travers to the abduction and murder of Cobby. Despite his youth, Travers had a long history of deviancy and violence. He was wanted for questioning in a sickening variety of sexual cases, which included both homosexual acts and the penetration of animals. Travers, who had been raised in wretched circumstances, was known to have tattoos etched on his penis. His dominating personality encouraged other unsavoury followers to replicate his acts of sexual violence.

He was wanted for questioning in a sickening variety of sexual cases...

Police soon believed that Travers, his ever loyal 19- year-old companion Mick Murdoch, and 24-year-old Les Murphy, had stolen the white Holden used in the abduction of Cobby. The trio admitted to car theft, but denied any knowledge about the young woman's rape and murder.

Further questioning also implicated 29-year-old Gary Murphy, and 34-year-old Michael Murphy in the homicide case, but little compelling information was gleaned from the five men, until crucial evidence was revealed from a woman dubbed "Miss X". She knew Travers well, and confided to police her belief that he was capable of committing a sex orientated murder.

...crucial evidence became available from a woman dubbed "Miss X".

The break through that police craved occurred when Travers admitted to "Miss X" that he murdered Cobby, and that her fate was sealed after she heard his name mentioned during the multiple sexual attacks she endured from the five men.

"We all talked about it," confided Travers to "Miss X", but I was the only one with the guts to do it."

From that point on the investigation took on a new momentum. Les Murphy revealed where the stolen car used in the abduction was hidden in Blacktown, and after Murdoch was arrested he confirmed that it was Travers who cut Cobby's throat.

All five were charged with abduction, rape and murder, and graphic details emerged about the perpetrators during their 12 week trial. The group had been drinking heavily and smoking marijuana, before randomly selecting their victim, and Cobby was constantly raped vaginally, anally and orally by all five abductors until Travers brutally ended her ordeal.

Travers pleaded guilty before the case was heard, and was not tried. The remaining four showed no remorse for their actions, and the court displayed no leniency. Loud applause broke out in the crowded courtroom, after they were found guilty and sentenced by Justice Victor Maxwell to life imprisonment for the term of their natural lives.

COPY CAT HORROR HOMICIDE

He could have been named after a cherub, but 14-year-old Bronson Blessington was far from angelic in his disposition.

Two years after this gruesome crime, the Sydney public was rocked again when 20 year-old Janine Balding was abducted, raped and murdered by a gang of five youths.

The gang members were a group of lowlifes and misfits, who lived on the streets and shared burgeoning careers in petty crime. They had only known each other a few hours before they abducted Balding, but in that short time a leader emerged in the group.

He could have been named after a cherub, but 14-year-old Bronson Blessington was far from angelic in his disposition. It was Blessington who suggested "getting a sheila and raping her", and the others enthusiastically supported the idea.

Blessington, who later became the latest serving long-term prisoner in New South Wales

Janine Balding

was raised in a deprived environment. As a boy he had been sexually abused by four male adults, and by the time he was 14 he was a street dwelling, alcoholic who frequently sniffed petrol.

One of Blesssington's willing followers was fifteen-year-old Wayne Wilmott, who had been in trouble with law enforcement agencies since the age of five. His girl friend of a few hours, 17-year-old Carol Ann Arrow, had run away from her home town of Leeton two years before. Sixteen-year-old Matthew Elliott was intellectually in the bottom 4% of the population, while the ape like features of the 23-year-old Stephen "Shorty" Jamieson, combined with his mental age of ten, resulted in him being an outcast in mainstream society.

While Wilmott drove the stolen car... Elliott raped Balding in the back seat at knife point.

On 8th August 1988, 20 year-old Janine Balding approached her car at the Sutherland railway station after finishing a day's work at the State Bank. The young woman from Wagga Wagga appeared to have the world at her feet. She was popular with work mates and had recently become engaged to be married, but the group that abducted her near her parked car tragically ended a life that was full of potential.

While Wilmott drove the stolen car down the F4 freeway with Arrow beside him, Elliott raped Balding in the back seat at knife point. When the vehicle stopped, the other males in the group raped her repeatedly, while Wilmott and Arrow enjoyed a sexual interlude in the nearby car. The helpless victim was then tied up and held face down in the water on the edge of the Minchinbury Dam until she drowned. Elliott later sold Balding's engagement ring, while the others used the deceased's credit card to steal $300 from an ATM outlet.

...tied up and held face down in the water on the edge of the Minchinbury Dam...

Soon after a social worker became suspicious about the behaviour of Blessington and Elliott, and she notified police about her concerns. The two teenagers made some admissions, and accompanied police to the dam where Balding's body was located. They, along with Wilmott and Arrow, claimed that the missing "Shorty" was responsible for the woman's death. Blessington added that Mark "Shorty" Wells was the full name of the culprit, but this known devil worshipper had a perfect alibi at the time the abduction and murder took place.

Fourteen days after the body was found, Stephen "Shorty" Jamieson was located in a Southport park on Queensland's Gold Coast. All of the five accused were arrested and charged with murder, but Wilmott and Arrow were later convicted of the lesser crimes of abduction and theft. Wilmott served ten years for these convictions while Arrow was given a custodial sentence of 18 months, and placed on a three-year good behaviour bond.

At a second trial in 1990, Jamieson, Blessington and Elliott showed no remorse, and Blessington frequently mouthed obscenities at the press gallery in the court room. All three were found guilty and sentenced to life sentence terms without parole. In his closing address, Judge Newman acknowledged the youth of the defendants, but felt that the seriousness of the offence ("one of the most barbaric killings in the sad criminal history of this state") justified the harsh penalty.

"one of the most barbaric killings in the sad criminal history of this state"

In custody Blessington has become a devour Christian and model prisoner, both he and Jamieson received unexpected support in recent times, when Peter Breen, and New South Wales upper-house member, publically supported their pleas of innocence.

In his book, "Life as a Sentence", Breen made what then NSW Premier Morris Jemma later described as "a sickening tribute", when he claimed that "I love Shorty Jamieson, I'm not afraid to say it".

Breen has since claimed that the Sydney print media misrepresented him, but shortly after his revelation Jemma persuaded him to resign from the Labor party.

Daryl Suckling

FROM THE MOUTH OF A VILLAIN

Daryl Francis Suckling could possibly have got away with murder, if he hadn't admitted his guilt to a gaol cellmate seven years after the homicide occurred.

In late December 1987, known prostitute and heroin addict Jodee Maree Larcombe, was reported missing after being released from Pentridge Prison. Three months later, in an unrelated incident, Sophie Carnic was abducted and assaulted by Daryl Suckling, a man who had racked up 138 criminal convictions since the age of 11.

...explicit photographs of a battered and bruised women...

During the assault and pornography sessions with Carnic, Suckling mentioned that he had murdered a woman, whom he later buried at a nearby property in Pooncarie. Police later found clothing, jewellery and explicit photographs of a battered and bruised women, and Suckling was charged with two murders.

Fortunately for the defendant, Carnic died of a drug overdose before the 1990 trial began, and without her evidence the case against Suckling for Larcombe's murder collapsed.

Larcombe's parents protested this decision, and they were strongly supported by community petitions. However the 58-year-old Suckling later "self destructed", as while he was serving time on a fraud charge, he confessed to a "wired" cell mate that it was he who killed Larcombe.

Jodee Larcombe's body was never found, but Daryl Francis Suckling was found guilty of her murder, and on 2nd September 1996 the hardened criminal was jailed for the term of his natural life.

HOMOPHOBIA MAYHEM

Homophobia has been a blight on mankind since biblical times. Relatively speaking, Australia has been a tolerant nation compared to Jamaica, which is arguably the gay-murder capital of the world, and a country where popular reggae artists openly support homosexual homicides. Saudi Arabia and the United States also have a poor history of tolerance. Perpetrators world-wide are likely to be gangs of teenagers or young men, and such offenders are also likely to act aggressively towards women.

...the gay-murder capital of the world...

Overall many Australians can feel little pride about their responses towards gay members of the population, and from 1989–90 the headland stretch of land between Bondi and

Tamarama beaches near Marks Park in Sydney, became an especially horrifying locality for homosexual attacks.

It is difficult to offer a rational explanation for the magnitude of savage assaults that were enacted against male members of Sydney's gay community over that two year period.

Was it a hang over from the recent "Grim Reaper" media campaign, or the result of long term and entrenched homophobia?

...three gay males were murdered on the cliffs of Bondi...

It was not until the 1970s that South Australia became the first state to de-criminalise homosexuality. NSW followed suit in 1984, and Tasmania, the most reluctant state, did not follow suit until 1997. Investigations into crimes against homosexuals were often incompetent, and in some case virtually non-existent. Incompetence or indifference was certainly the hallmarks of some poor policing around a beach suburb area that became known to the gay community as the "Bondi Badlands".

Violence in that area towards homosexuals had become endemic. By the late '80s and early '90s, three gay males were murdered on the cliffs of Bondi, while five others perished in the inner city area. However it was the July 1989 disappearance of popular Wollongong news and weather reader Ross Warren that finally revealed the full extent of the horrifying practice of "poofter" bashing.

On the night of 21st July 1989, 25-year-old Ross Warren enjoyed a long night's socialising with friends before driving to the headland at South Bondi, a well known "pick up" place for gay men. At 2.45 am he was observed walking towards Marks Park. He then vanished.

...neither Warren's car or his car keys were finger printed...

Next evening worried friends found Warren's parked car near Tamarama Beach, and by Monday morning they found the missing man's car keys on the rocky staircase leading to the McKenzie Bay foreshore. By Tuesday media outlets reported that Ross Warren was missing.

The ineptitude that characterised many crimes involving homosexuals soon permeated the investigation. As days went by, neither Warren's car or his car keys were finger printed, and no photographs were taken of the crime scene. This unsolved case gathered dust for another 11 years, and no inquest was held during that time.

No further action may have occurred, in this virtually forgotten case, if Warren's mother had not sparked the interest of Detective Sergeant Stephen Page. He soon discovered that all of the young man's friends believed Ross Warren had been murdered. Former investigating officers had dismissed it as a disappearance or suicide case, even though two similar deaths followed within a year of Warren vanishing.

...the lump of hair that Russell clutched in his hand as he died, disappeared from police custody.

Page came to believe that there was a pattern to these deaths and other attacks. He received little initial support in these views, even though one of the victims, (Thai national Kritchikom Rattanajuraithaporn), was virtually tortured to death, and the corpse of John Russell was found with clumps of someone's hair held tightly in his hand.

Again police response to this crime was disappointing. At first they believed that Russell had fallen from the cliff's edge, despite bad cuts and bruises to the victim's face. The first inquest found that the former Sydney barman had died from misadventure.

Page later discovered that police laundered the clothes of the deceased man, in order to later dress an identikit model for identification purposes. This resulted in any DNA evidence being obliterated, when similar clothing would clearly have been a better option. Finally, the lump of hair that Russell clutched in his hand as he died, disappeared from police custody

The determined Page kept on following leads, and he finally identified three groups that habitually terrorised members of the gay community. One group originated from Cleveland High School, and they were known as the "Alexandria Eight". This teenage gang killed at least one person. Another group was nicknamed the

"Tamarama Three", and their main victim was the Thai national. Finally there were the "Bondi Boys", who bashed many and attempted to kill a future key witness. The gangs mostly operated independently of each other.

...savagely bashed the victim with a claw hammer...

Page's investigations of the "Tamarma Three" focussed especially on the attack on Geoffrey Sullivan in July 1990. Seventeen-year-old Sean McAuliffe, his 16-year-old brother David, and 16-year-old Matthew Davies, set out from Redfern that evening to "roll a poof". At McKenzies Point they accosted Sullivan, and after demanding money, Sean McAuliffe savagely bashed the victim with a claw hammer until he was unconscious. Sullivan was left seriously injured by the trio, who returned to Redfern to "smoke a bong".

Davies later boasted to his mates about the gang's exploits, and crucial information was then relayed to police by the mother of one of the young thug's friends. After being arrested and tried, the McAuliffe brothers received 20 years in custody with a non-parole period of 12 years, while Davies was gaoled for 19 years with a minimum of 11 years.

The Warren disappearance and the Russell murder remained unsolved, despite Page's growing belief that Sean Leigh Cushman, the ringleader of the "Bondi Boys", was a key suspect in both crimes. In 1996 Cushman and Aaron

Martin were arrested over the assault and death of a 28-year-old English visitor. Surprisingly, both received a good behaviour bond for the attack that many witnesses had viewed.

The Sydney victims were not dangerous bank robbers, or enemies of organised crime.

Page's persistence on these cold cases finally resulted in an inquest being conducted on 31st March 2003, and in May 2005, five years after Page first commenced his investigations, the coronial findings damned initial police investigations into both the Warren and Russell cases.

The Deputy State Coroner, Justice Jacqueline Milledge, stated in her final summary that

"All I can do is urge communities... to regard victimisation of a gay man or lesbian, as completely abhorrent and not to be tolerated."

The Sydney victims were not dangerous bank robbers, or enemies of organised crime. They had no criminal records, and died because they sought consensual sex from other gay men.

Stephen Page no longer serves in the NSW police force. The devoted husband and family man received a death threat before the 2003 inquest began, and he has since resigned and started his own lawn mowing and security business.

POOR MAN'S NED

Edwin Street never became a criminal legend like Ned Kelly, but after he was sentenced he at least emulated the folk hero in his comments.

Street's de facto wife Dawn was a charity worker who cared for quadriplegics, but on 17th December 1993 the 42-year-old woman went missing for 18 days. She was then found buried in a large shopping bag in a Sydney park.

Then, on 23rd February 1994, investigating police came across the corpse of Street's new de facto wife, Linda Whitton, in a bag at his Elmore home. The officers had asked Street for a bag to take away some items of clothing that belonged to Street's deceased first partner, but when they opened the bag they discovered the second body.

...but when they opened the bag they discovered the second body.

Street explained that Linda Whitton had stabbed herself several times before he could wrest the knife from her, but the disbelieving investigators noted that one of the stab wounds was in her back.

At Street's trial on 29th June 1995, details of his many previous sexual convictions were

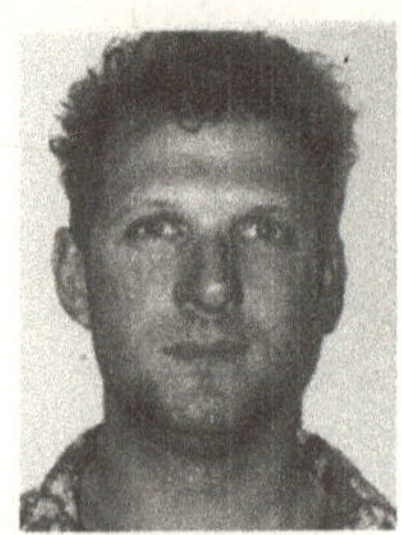
Leslie Camilleri

revealed, and he received the maximum sentence for murdering the two small, frail women.

As he was led from the court Street echoed the words of the legendary Ned Kelly when he commented

"Such is life."

TRAGIC END TO TEENAGE PRANKS

Unfortunately, the two men were the worst kind of sexual predators.

It was typical teenage girls' antics – daringly indulging in a couple of illegal drinks, before rashly deciding to embark on a lonely evening walk along the Snowy Mountain Highway to a friend's house. Accepting a lift in a car from two male strangers, fitted in well with the independent adult image they wished to convey. Unfortunately, the two men who either lured or forced them into a car around 10 pm on 4th October 1997 were the worst kind of sexual predators.

The Collins and Barry families had become close friends after settling on the NSW South Coast at Kalaru near Bega, and 14-year-old Lauren Barry and 16-year-old Nichole Collins became constant companions.

Nichole Collins consumed two glasses of bourbon and coke to celebrate an approaching birthday on that early October evening, but that same night the pair disappeared.

Three days later Lauren's semen-stained shirt was found near the old Walagoot Road tip at Bega, but it was the only definite clue the task force search party came across for the next three weeks. Reports filtered through to police about a cream and yellow sedan car being sighted in the Tathra area around the time the girls disappeared, but nothing initially came from these reports. No-one was then aware that the two men travelling in the vehicle were repeat sex offenders whom the court system had injudiciously set free, despite the obvious risks they represented to society.

Lindsay Beckett

...six charges of sexual penetration against an 11-year-old girl.

Twenty-eight-year-old Leslie Camilleri's criminal record stretched back 16 years, and he had already been connected with 215 vehicle related offences, as well as 92 convictions for stealing. More importantly, Camilleri's alleged record of sex offences, was dangerously relevant in connection with the missing teenage girls.

Camilleri had recently appeared in the Queanbeyan Court before Judge Fred Kirkman, to answer six charges of sexual penetration against an 11-year-old girl. Shortly before the trial began, the then NSW Police Minister made strong public statements about the conviction of sex offenders, which Camilleri's legal representatives argued were extraordinary and prejudicial to their client's right to a fair trial. Judge Kirkman declared the case aborted, and Camilleri was released on bail.

The other culprit, 23-year-old New Zealand- born Lindsay Beckett, also had repeat convictions for sexual crimes and theft. On the 13th September 1997, the dangerous duo reportedly raped a woman in Canberra, but no charges were pressed.

Beckett held Nichole's head under water before slashing her throat savagely with a knife.

On the October night the teenage girls disappeared, Camilleri and Beckett were travelling to Bega to visit Camilleri's de facto wife. After persuading or forcing the girls into their car, the predatory duo repeatedly raped them for the next nine hours while travelling west, before debating how they would kill their victims. Finally, after Lauren was first tied to a tree, Beckett held Nichole's head under water in Fiddlers Green Creek before slashing her throat savagely with a knife.

After Lauren was disposed of in the same brutal manner the murderers drove to Canberra, where they threw the knife from Commonwealth Bridge into Lake Burleigh Griffin. Beckett's blood stained clothes were then burnt, and the car was thoroughly cleaned. Soon after the pair were gaoled on unrelated charges, before police questioned them about the missing teenagers.

It was Beckett who finally admitted to killing the innocent girls with Camilleri, and on

12th November he accompanied police to where the two bodies were located 15 metres apart. The murder weapon was recovered by police divers next day, and on 19th November over 4,000 people attended a memorial service for the girls in Bega.

On 27th April 1999, Lindsay Beckett received a life sentence with a non-parole period of 35 years, while Leslie Camilleri received the same sentence with no specified parole period.

HERO TURNED VILLAIN

On 18th January 1987, Sydney witnessed carnage on an enormous scale, when 83 people were killed and 220 others injured after a peak hour train accidentally struck a bridge pylon, which brought tonnes of concrete crashing down on helpless travellers.

...he was a cold blooded standover man and hired killer...

One of the heroes of this Granville train disaster was Lindsay Thomas Rose, a paramedic who risked his life to rescue and comfort many injured people. There was also a dangerously dark side to Rose's character; he was a cold blooded standover man and hired killer, who finally admitted to murdering five people.

In 1984 he shot and killed 58-year-old Edward Kavanagh and his 21-year-old girlfriend Carmelita

Lee. Three years later he stabbed to death Reynette Holford, after she interrupted an attempted house robbery, and in 1994 he shot and stabbed two Sydney prostitutes. Rose received $20,000 from the husband of 36-year-old Kerrie Pang for her execution, but Fatima Oronzal was shot dead because she was an unlucky witness to Pang's murder.

Rose received $20,000 from the husband of 36-year-old Kerrie Pang for her execution...

Ronald Lewis Waters accompanied Rose when this double homicide took place, but the murder case against him was later dismissed. Rose was forced to live a life on the run for nine months after a disgraced detective friend submitted his name to a NSW Crime Commission, but he was finally arrested in Adelaide, and extradited to Sydney in April 1997.

On 3rd September 1998, Lindsay Thomas Rose was sentenced to life imprisonment with no non-parole period.

CONSUMED WITH JEALOUSY

Jason Mark Murphy and Malyssa Mackay were involved in a tempestuous relationship for two years, before Mackay ended their involvement, and moved with her three children to a caravan park in the Melbourne suburb of Sunshine.

Murphy was still committed to the relationship, and he soon financed the family's relocation to an established house. However Mackay had met and become engaged to 34-year-old Christopher Jewel when she resided at the caravan park, and Murphy became so consumed with jealousy when Jewel also became a resident at the house, that he threatened to kill his rival.

Mackay did not take the threats of her 29-year-old ex-boyfriend seriously, but she agreed to have sex with him twice in a bid to stop his continual harassment and stalking activities.

Her ploy initially appeared to be successful, but on 18th July 2000 Murphy and fellow bouncer Clive Clayton Watson donned balaclavas and abducted Jewel. Their victim was handcuffed, and had his eyes and mouth covered with tape. After his wallet and mobile phone were stolen, Jewel was driven 50 kilometres from Sunshine to Lerderderg State Park near Bacchus Marsh, where he was bundled into the boot of his car.

...fire-fighters found the handcuffed and charred body...

That same day Murphy hid a bag containing a sawn off shot gun, two balaclavas, a pillow case and gloves with a friend, who was also asked to provide him with an alibi. Watson was unsuccessful when he attempted to withdraw $1,000 from Jewel's account at an ATM outlet, as the balance was only $30.

Next day the two abductors returned to Jewel's car and set it on fire, even though their victim may still have been alive. Later that same day, CFA fire-fighters found the handcuffed and charred body of Jewel in the back of his vehicle.

On 6th September 2001, Murphy received a 22-year life sentence for the murder of Jewel, while Watson was convicted of manslaughter and placed in custody for eight years. In a bizarre twist, it was revealed in court that Mackay had penned sexually explicit letters to Murphy after Jewel perished. Mackay claimed that the letters were a ploy which aimed to uncover the true circumstances of her fiancée's death.

DEALING WITH FAMILY PROBLEMS

Nicola Spira was never popular with his in-laws, who were often critical about the argumentative 28-year-old marriage relationship he shared with 49-year-old Maria. Nicola's dealings with his 73-year-old mother-in-law, Giovanna, and his brother-in-law, Faustino, were also fractious.

On the evening of Saturday 21st October 2001, 55-year-old Nicola was allegedly being physically assaulted by his wife and mother-in-law, and he battered them to death when he defended himself from their hits and bites. Their bodies were deposited in his garage, and Nicola

...he battered them to death when he defended himself from their hits and bites.

then cleaned up the blood spattered house, before showering and hanging out the freshly washed clothes that had been soiled during the assault.

Next day he continued tidying the house, before ringing his brother-in-law and persuading him to pay a visit. Faustino arrived on Sunday afternoon around 3.40 pm, and for the next four hours he was held hostage at gunpoint by Nicola. During this time he was unaware of his mother's and sister's fate, but he finally managed to dial emergency 000, and leave his threatening captor. Nicola Spira was arrested by police shortly afterwards, as he drove towards Springvale Cemetery with the bodies of the two women in the boot of his car.

...the dead women had been slowly strangled...

Much damning evidence against the accused was found. Only superficial wounds were sustained from the alleged vicious attack on him, it was revealed that the dead women had been slowly strangled, and a blood stained rope containing the old woman's DNA was found in the boot of Spira's car. There were also blood stains discovered on a billiard cue in the accused man's house, and his wife's head had been struck at least eight times with a blunt object.

Police believed that Maria Spira was actually murdered on 19th October, and her mother suffered the same fate a day later. They also suspected that Nicola Spira's two brothers-in-law were the next two homicide targets. The main motives for Nicola Spira's murderous assaults were greed and revenge. He regarded Maria as being a spendthrift, and he hated her family for the many years they had ostracised him.

Nicola Spira was sentenced to four life terms for two murders, threatening to kill and false imprisonment. His non-parole period is 25 years, and appeals against the severity of his sentence have currently been unsuccessful.

A PREVIOUSLY DISREGARDED CRIME

Stalking, whether in person or digital, has long been a serious crime. Current statistics show that one in five women and one in thirteen men have experienced stalking in their lifetime. However, 85% of stalkers are male. Offences are often not reported, and most victims suffer substantial angst and horror from their nerve wracking experiences. Identification of the culprits is usually reasonably simple, but gaining sufficient evidence is more problematic.

Stalkers seek to control and torture their victims by constantly watching, following and intimidating their prey.

Stalkers seek to control and torture their victims by constantly watching, following and intimidating their prey. They become consumed by their obsessions, and their collective and community responsibilities deteriorate. Victims often become alienated from their customary support base

Stalkers are a plague in our society. They cannot be dismissed as unimportant pests, and they need to be detected and apprehended before their obsessive behaviour escalates into physical violence.

UNRELENTING HARASSMENT

It was easy for "Hopkins" to discover her new location, as he had tapped her phone...

One typical real life situation was methodically documented by author Chris Smith in his book "Stalked". The male stalker, "Phillip Hopkins", often donned a balaclava and crept around "Libby Masters'" residence at night. He would further intimidate his ex-lover by shining his torch at the building, rattling windows and throwing objects against the house.

When the distraught victim reported his behaviour to local police in 1995, it was treated as an exaggerated "beat up", and a waste of time and resources for a woman who was virtually treated as being a public nuisance. "Libby's" work performances suffered due to increasing bouts of insomnia, and she moved back to her parents' home. It was easy for "Hopkins" to discover her

One former girlfriend even fled overseas in order to escape his remorseless and unwanted attentions.

new location, as he had tapped her phone, so the harassment continued unabated. The huge problem was made more difficult by the sceptical attitude of "Libby's" father to the situation. His apparent disbelief was mirrored by the magistrate to whom she applied to have an Aggravated Violence Order (AVO) placed against "Hopkins".

"Libby Masters" became so desperate that she contemplated murdering her ex-lover, with whom she had previously shared a passionate but unpredictable relationship. During their time together, "Hopkins" became increasingly violent towards her, and these instances of aggressive behaviour were invariably followed by remorseful apologies and pleas for chances of redemption. Sudden absences and failures to keep appointments, placed further stains on their relationship.

Later it was revealed that "Hopkins" was a serial offender, and during his unexplained absences from "Masters" he was stalking previous lovers and new targets. One former girlfriend even fled overseas in order to escape his remorseless and unwanted attentions.

Finally "Libby Masters" received valued support from the TV program "A Current Affair", and the stalker's crimes were exposed to the public. Following these revelations, many other females came forward with incriminating evidence against the offender, with some cases occurring ten years before the television exposure of "Hopkins".

At first his parents and he either denied the accusations or rationalised the problem, but finally "Hopkins" served a custodial sentence of a year for his stalking activities. Following his release "Hopkins" did make one final unlawful attempt to contact "Libby Masters", but most recent reports suggest that the problem has been resolved. Both the perpetrator and the victim now live in new locations in stable married relationships that have produced children.

GOLDEN DAYS END

...the wheels fell off Gary Neiwand's cycling career shortly after the completion of the Sydney 2000 Olympics.

He was a former world champion, Olympic Games silver medallist and multiple Commonwealth Games medallist, but the wheels comprehensively fell off Gary Neiwand's cycling career shortly after the completion of the Sydney 2000 Olympic Games. The champion athlete and father of two, was said then to be suffering from depression over his marriage break up, which may have contributed to the multiple stalking crimes he committed.

Over a few catastrophic months Neiwand became a serial offender, harassing a former girlfriend as well as four other women with sexually explicit and abusive phone calls or text messages. He also stole a mobile phone as well as other items, and breached an intervention order that was taken out by his ex-girlfriend.

...pleaded guilty to five cases of stalking, two of theft, three of using a phone in a harassing manner...

On 28th July 2006, Neiwand pleaded guilty to five cases of stalking, two of theft, three of using a phone in a harassing manner and one for breaching an intervention order. He was sentenced to 18 months gaol with a minimum term of nine months.

Victorian Chief Magistrate Ian Gray, who handed down Neiwand's sentence, believed that the chances of rehabilitation for Neiwand were strong. He was impressed by the former champion cyclist's acceptance of his problems, and the level of good family support that is available to him.

CHAPTER FOUR:

THOSE WHO PREY ON CHILDREN

SECOND CHANCE DISASTER IN QUEENSLAND

Child murderer Barry Gordon Hadlow was sentenced to life imprisonment with hard labour, for the sexual molestation and killing of nine-year-old Stacey Ann Tracey, in the west Queensland town of Roma on 22nd May 1990.

The jury that convicted him was unaware that he committed an almost identical murder 28 years before that Roma atrocity. In the public domain, the majority of citizens angrily rejected the excuses provided by the Queensland Corrective Services Commission, and Hadlow's former parole officer, for releasing him after his previous child killing.

Before the 1962 homicide in Townsville was solved, the quietly spoken Hadlow appeared to be full of compassion to the Bacon family, when their five-year-old

...shoved the little girl's body into a sack...

daughter Sandra Dorothy disappeared. The 20-year-old labourer assisted in the search for the missing girl, and he expressed the opinion that the child may have been murdered and her body placed in a car boot. His forecast proved to be chillingly accurate.

The overweight and socially rejected Hadlow, whose known criminal activities began at the age of 16, had shoved the little girl's body into a sack and hidden her corpse in a car boot, after he had stabbed her with a hunting knife. Prior to her murder, the child had been sent to fetch her older sister, before Hadlow lured her into his nearby home with the promise of a comic book. Inside his premises, he sexually assaulted Sandra Dorothy Bacon before strangling and stabbing her. When police interviewed him later that day, Hadlow appeared almost boastful when he readily confessed to the appalling crime.

A psychiatrist predicted that Hadlow would readily re-offend if he was not kept in a place of safety, but in gaol the convicted man appeared to rehabilitate his life. He became a devout Christian, and the model prisoner was released after serving 22 years.

Shortly after he was freed in 1985, Hadlow married Leonie Moodie who had eight children from a previous marriage. He informed his new wife about his dark past, and she believed that he was a reformed man. The couple moved to Roma, where Hadlow gained employment as a store packer at the local supermarket. When drunk, he would regale his workmates with tales about his prison experiences, and reports of these anecdotes brought police to his house soon after nine-year-old Stacey Ann Tracey disappeared on 22nd May 1990.

The pattern of Hadlow's behaviour was chillingly similar to his Townsville murder. Four days after she went missing, he joined the search party which discovered the girl's body in scrub country. The victim had been sexually assaulted, and her corpse partially wrapped in a green plastic garbage bag. However in her hand was a torn scrap of paper, which fitted into a ripped sample that was later found at Hadlow's residence.

...her corpse partially wrapped in a green plastic garbage bag.

After he received his life sentence, Hadlow maintained that police had framed him for the killing because of his previous conviction. His appeal fell on deaf ears, and in July 2007 the 65-year-old Hadlow died in a Brisbane hospital, after complaining of shortness of breath while in custody.

RELEASE UNLIKELY IN VICTORIA

...a serial child killer who will never be set free.

Queensland may well have erred when it released Barry Hadlow in 1985, but Victorian authorities appear unlikely to ever give Derek Ernest Percy a similar chance of freedom.

The chilling series of murders by the state's longest serving prisoner have been well documented in the past, and recent revelations about the paedophile's crimes have only strengthened the belief that Derek Percy is a serial child killer who will never be set free.

Shortly before his 21st birthday in 1969, Percy tortured and horribly mutilated 12-year-old Yvonne Tuohy at Warneet on Victoria's Westernport Bay near the HMAS Cerberus base, where the outwardly unremarkable young man was then stationed in the Australian navy. Authorities now believe that the murder of Yvonne Tuohy was only one of many killings committed by Percy in various parts of the country.

Percy's father, who was employed in the State Electricity Commission (SEC), was a yachting enthusiast who took his family with him when he attended various interstate regattas during his annual holidays. His teenage son was therefore present in far flung locations, when horrifying and often unsolved crimes were committed.

In January 1965 the then 16-year-old Percy was in Sydney with his family when Marianne Schmidt and Mary Sharrock were murdered. The mutilated bodies of the two teenage neighbours were found at Wanda Beach near Cronulla. This gruesome double murder case has never been solved, but an identikit photo of a youth seen talking to the two girls earlier that day, closely resembles Percy.

Percy was also in Adelaide when the three Beaumont children went missing on Australia Day in 1966, and he was holidaying in Canberra when six-year-old Allen Redson was abducted and murdered. A description of a young cyclist observed near the Canberra murder scene, closely resembled a teenage Derek Percy.

An entry in Percy's diary graphically details the fatal injuries inflicted on the baby boy.

The Percy link to unsolved killings around the nation continued. Nearly seven month after Percy enlisted in the navy, three-year-old Simon Brook was abducted and murdered in the inner Sydney suburb of Glebe. An entry in Percy's diary graphically details the fatal injuries inflicted on the baby boy.

Derek Percy was on leave in Melbourne when Linda Stillwell was abducted and murdered near the St. Kilda foreshore, and shortly before Yvonne Tuohy was slain, a 12-year-old girl narrowly escaped abduction from a young man near the Cerberus base. She later identified Percy as the culprit.

This predatory paedophile is now nearly 60, and he has served almost 40 years in custody. Recent revelations about his sinister past suggest that he will remain in prison until he dies.

There is no rationale explanation for Derek Percy's evil activities. He was raised in a stable middle class home and is highly intelligent. His promising school results plummeted shortly after bizarre sexual fantasies began to appear in his diary entries. However when his concerned parents sought their family doctor's advice, they were assured that the disturbing images he wrote about were only puberty fantasies that would not last.

...stealing women's underwear from a neighbour's clothes line...

Around that time the Mt. Beauty secondary student was suspected of stealing women's underwear from a neighbour's clothes line, and Percy also slashed items of women's clothing with a knife. Soon after his family moved to Khancoban, Derek Percy attempted to molest a four-year-old girl.

During his decades in prison, Derek Percy has been a self sufficient inmate, who has shunned all professional help for his unusual paedophile condition. As recently as 1998, Justice Eames refused his application to be released back into mainstream society, and this decision is likely to be replicated in the future, following the July 2007 discovery of potentially damaging new evidence.

Police obtained a court order to seize 35 boxes of files that had been concealed by Percy in a South Melbourne self-storage warehouse since the early 1970s. The pictures of children, hand written diaries, razor blades and videos that were uncovered, may help link Percy to other child abductions and murders that occurred in the 1960s.

Percy was expected to face further police questioning about unsolved murder cases once the new warehouse evidence was comprehensively reviewed. However, Percy died from lung cancer in 2013 having served 44 of his 64 years in gaol.

CAUTIOUS ATTITUDE IN NSW

...murdered five-year-old Nicole in bed at her home after stabbing her 17 times.

John David Lewthwaite is regarded by many as being an intractable homosexual paedophile. The convicted child killer has had a long and currently unsuccessful battle to be released back into mainstream society.

On 26th June 1974, Lewthwaite savagely murdered five–year–old Nicole Margaret Hanns in bed at her home after stabbing her 17 times.

John David Lewthwaite

Lewthwaite's sexual target was actually her 11-year-old brother Anthony, and he angrily killed the boy's little sister when she awoke before Lewthwaite reached his prey.

The murderer, who was then also facing arson charges, exposed himself next day to a group of schoolboys at North Sydney. Lewthwaite then unsuccessfully attempted to confess his crime at three different churches, before he contacted his parole officer and later surrendered to police. At the time Anthony Hanns and both his parents were prime suspects in the murder case, and all had been questioned extensively before Lewthwaite was arrested and later sentenced to life imprisonment.

...escaped from custody in both 1975 and 1985...

Lewthwaite escaped from custody in both 1975 and 1985, when he absconded from a psychiatric hospital and Long Bay gaol respectively, which renewed police fears about Anthony Hanns' safety. Later Hann's family, and many in the general public, expressed disgust when it became known that the 1985 escape resulted from an unaccompanied visit to a psychiatrist in the city. The Hanns were understandably traumatised by the cavalier attitude of authorities in regard to Anthony's safety, and received $20,000 compensation from the state government.

Worse news was in store for Lewthwaite's

many detractors. In July 1992 the now deeply religious prisoner, had his sentence reduced to a minimum of 20 years, and he was transferred to the low security Cooma gaol where he was eligible for day release passes.

This change created furore in state parliament and the general community. Some politicians sought amendments in the Sentencing Act which would allow the Crown to appeal such decisions, but opponents such as the Uniting Church, believed these independent procedures should not be subjected to interference. The murder victim's mother, Gwen Hanns, lobbied strongly against any leniency. Ultimately the Offenders' Review Board decreed that a monthly day release program would apply for Lewthwaite.

Lewthwaite indulged himself in nude sunbathing at Sydney's Wanda beach.

On 6th October 1995 he was formally refused parole. In Long Bay gaol Lewthwaite broke 23 years of public silence about his conviction, declaring that politics was keeping him in prison. He also said that he was now no longer a paedophile, an opinion that is supported by his long term partner Brian Craig, whom he first met in custody.

Lewthwaite was finally released from prison in 1999, but seven years later he was back in custody after being charged with willful and obscene exposure.

Lewthwaite indulged himself in nude sunbathing at Sydney's Wanda beach. Magistrate William Brydon later concluded that Lewthwaite's actions were not offensive, as he was only observed by police. He was, however, returned to custody for breaching his bail conditions.

PINK WAS HER FAVOURITE COLOUR

...her decomposed was found stuffed in a storm water drain...

It was a cold winter morning on 29th June 1991, when six-year-old Sheree Beasley donned her pink bicycle helmet, and rode her much loved pink bicycle, towards a corner shop in Rosebud to purchase some supplies for her mother. She then disappeared, and three months later her decomposed body was found stuffed in a storm water drain 15 kilometres from where she was last seen.

A witness on that day recalled seeing someone in a Toyota Corolla hatchback picking up a little girl who answered Sheree's description. All owners of such cars in the state were contacted by police, and investigators particularly remembered the curt manner of one Corolla owner.

The man in question declared that he had no connection with that area of the Mornington Peninsula, and that he had been involved in family activities on the day in question, at his home in the Melbourne suburb of Glen

Waverley. His abrupt replies to routine questions attracted further interest from the investigating team, who made further enquiries about Robert Arthur Selby Lowe.

Lowe appeared to be a model of middle class respectability. He was a salesman who was conservative in his appearance and habits, he was married with two sons, and he devoted much time to community projects. Both his wife and he were strongly involved with their local church, where he was a Sunday school teacher. However he lied unnecessarily when he denied any connection with Rosebud, as the Lowes owned an often used holiday flat in that bay-side area. Further research by police revealed that Lowe had a murky criminal past.

"he truly believes that he is indulging in harmless behaviour"

Robert Arthur Selby Lowe was born in England in 1937, and his family moved first to New Zealand before he settled in Australia. In all three counties Lowe amassed a series of convictions for stealing, exposing himself in public, and indecent assault. He served two jail terms in New Zealand before relocating to Australia. In his new abode Lowe found solace in religion, and in 1972 he married Lorraine Sangster, who was also a devout Christian. She only learned about her husband's disturbing past life after Sheree Beasley disappeared.

In the six years from 1984-1990, Lowe committed further minor sexual offences, and during that time he came to rely heavily on the advice and guidance of his psychotherapist, Margaret Hobbs. In a written report about his crimes, Hobbs noted that "he (Lowe) truly believes that he is indulging in harmless behaviour... when his behaviour is obviously unacceptable."

After Sheree Beasley was reported missing, a concerned Hobbs provided information to police, who interviewed Lowe exhaustively. Initially he was released without charge, but other pressures in his life were beginning to impact on Lowe. His employment was terminated, and he moved to the Rosebud flat after his wife failed to support his alibi about being at home in Glen Waverley on the day the little girl vanished.

...the convicted "lifer" had no respect for child killers.

On 24th September Sheree's body was found, and Lowe was arrested and charged, largely because of the circumstantial evidence that Hobbs provided. New convincing evidence was vitally needed for a conviction to be made, and the break-through came from a completely unexpected source.

Police murderer Peter Allan Reid was a fellow inmate of Lowe's in K division of Pentridge Gaol, and the convicted "lifer" had no respect for child killers. He volunteered to relay any relevant information about the Beasley case that he gleaned from his conversations with Lowe, and the secret tactic fortunately paid dividends.

Lowe divulged to Reid how he stalked and abducted his chosen victim, before the little girl choked to death when he forced her to provide oral sex. After she died, Lowe callously disposed of her body in the storm water drain.

His trial began in late 1994, and Reid's accumulated evidence proved so damaging that a jury found Lowe guilty after five hours deliberation. The evidence presented was so graphic, that Justice Cummins was reduced to tears when he handed down a life sentence to Lowe for the murder of Sheree Beasley. At one stage Lowe was also a suspect for the murder of six-year-old Kylie Maybury, before DNA evidence cleared him of guilt.

EBONY'S LEGACY

Ebony's school bag was filled with rocks... threw her into the waters of the dam.

Ebony Simpson alighted from the school bus in her small home town of Bargo on the afternoon of 19th August 1992. On the 400 metre stroll to her home, she walked near a short, thin man who appeared to be tinkering with the engine of his old car. Violence then erupted out of nowhere in the tranquil rural surroundings. Ebony was seized by her predator, thrown into the boot of the parked

Andrew Peter Garforth

car and driven to a dam seven kilometres away.

There the child predator bound his victim's hands and feet with wire before sexually abusing her. Ebony's school bag was filled with rocks, which caused her to sink quickly when the 29-year-old father of two boys secured the bag to her back, and threw her into the waters of the dam. By the time the little girl drowned, Andrew Peter Garforth was driving back to his home.

Next day Garforth joined a volunteer search group of 150, but before long police received illuminating reports about his recent behaviour. A male driving an old car in poor condition, who answered the unemployed labourer's description, had regularly been sighted following school buses. Garforth admitted his guilt after he was apprehended and showed investigating officers where he drowned Ebony Simpson. Police divers recovered the girl's body two days after she was abducted.

At his trial an angry crowd of about 200 people yelled abuse and hurled missiles at Garforth, when he was escorted under police guard into the courtrooms. Since receiving a life imprisonment sentence without parole on 9th July 1993, the despised child killer has also been attacked by prisoners at both Long Bay and Goulburn gaols. Two appeals against the severity of his 40-year sentence have been dismissed.

...the despised child killer has also been attacked by prisoners at gaols.

Following their daughter's murder, Christine and Peter Simpson have provided a lasting legacy for Ebony, by establishing the Homicide Victim's Support Group (HVSG), which serves needy people from far flung locations. Over 600 families in NSW alone have received help, and this support was extended to international families of the Belangalo State Forest murder victims in the 1990s, with accommodation being provided for the overseas travellers at Ebony House. Financial compensation for families of victims is now more generous, a Charter of Victim's Rights has been implemented, and annual government subsidies of $250,000 are made available to the HVSG.

WAS JUSTICE SERVED?

Kathleen Folbigg is currently serving a 64 year sentence, with a minimum non parole period of 30 years, after being found guilty of murdering her four children in the late 1990s. In 2007 the 40-year-old Folbigg lost what is probably her last chance of repeal, when the NSW Supreme Court rejected another appeal against her verdict. In response to a petition presented by Folbigg's supporters, in August 2018, the NSW Attorney General announced an inquiry into her convictions. The subsequent report found no reason-

...being found guilty of murdering her four children in the late 1990s.

Kathleen Folbigg

able doubt as to the guilt of Folbigg. However, in March 2021, 90 prominent scientists called for Kathleen Folbigg to be pardoned as they published evidence that a rare genetic condition may have caused the deaths of two of her children. Her lawyers have launched a new appeal in the NSW courts.

In a similar case in Victoria on 25th October 2007, four infant homicide charges against Carol Matthey were dismissed by the Victorian Supreme Court. Evidence presented against Matthey then was finally ruled to be inadmissible.

...stopped breathing after she fell off a coffee table.

The deaths of Carol Matthey's children began on 8th December 1998, when she discovered the deceased body of her seven-month- old son Jacob in his cot. Sudden Infant Death Syndrome (SIDS) was the official cause of death.

Eleven months later her ten-week-old daughter Chloe also died of SIDS, and on 10th July 2002, Joshua Matthey stopped breathing, in his pram, at a shopping centre car-park. At the time the eight-week-old boy was receiving medical treatment for an ear infection, and it was ruled that he died from Klebsiella Septicernia.

Just over two years later, Carol Matthey summoned an ambulance to her Geelong home when her three-year-old daughter Shania reportedly stopped breathing after she fell off a coffee table. The girl was breathing and conscious when the paramedics arrived at the accident scene, but next morning she was found dead in her bed. This fatality was declared "unascertained", and an exhaustive police investigation began into the causes of the multiple deaths.

Evidence was painstakingly gathered by investigating officers over the next three years, and 160 witnesses were interviewed. However the case against Carol Matthey never went to trial, after key evidence was decreed to be inadmissible.

...was very rare for four infant deaths to occur within the same family over a five-year-period.

In legal terms the judgement was not an acquittal, and if new evidence emerges another trial could be called. Previously, at Matthey's committal hearing in March 2006, her defence team, as well as forensic and pathology experts, argued that there was no physical evidence of harm to any of the deceased children, and that all the deaths possibly resulted from a shared and at present undiscovered genealogical defect.

The prosecution on the other hand stressed that the wife felt very insecure in her troubled marriage, and that there had been a series of other life threatening episodes due to shoddy parental practices. Furthermore, it was very rare for four infant deaths to occur within the same family over a five-year-period. They also suggested that Carol Matthey appeared to be indifferent about her children's deaths, but this opinion was strongly disputed by her support group.

A comparison of the Folbigg and Matthey cases is illuminating. Folbigg's four children died over a ten-year-period, and Matthey's offspring were deceased within five years. Both women felt insecure with their marriage partners, though Craig Folbigg strongly supported his wife's innocence when each of his children died.

The essential difference in available evidence was the discovery of Kathleen Folbigg's tortured diary entries, which strongly indicated her guilt. No similar "hard" evidence has currently surfaced in the Carol Matthey investigation.

"The only winner is the justice system" was how Matthey's defence lawyer, Paul Lacava, reportedly summarised the vexed case.

How can anyone declare that justice has been served, when the deaths of four children from the one family remain unresolved?

"take away the things that mean the most to her"

HUSBAND'S REVENGE

In August 2005, Greg King met Robert Farquharson outside a fish and chip shop in the Victorian town of Winchelsea. Life had become difficult for King's old friend. He was receiving medical attention for depression following the break-up of his marriage, and his former wife continued to be a financial burden to him. She had legal custody of their three sons, and a new man had entered her life. The bitter Farquharson reportedly threatened to "take away the things that mean the most to her", and that his plan would involve the three children on a special occasion, so that their mother would always suffer on that anniversary day.

Robert Farquharson

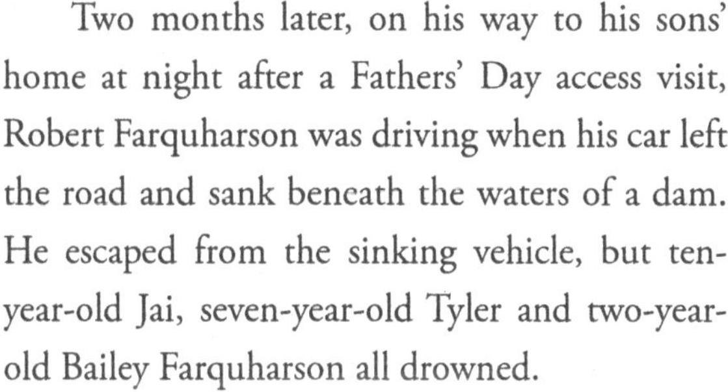

Two months later, on his way to his sons' home at night after a Fathers' Day access visit, Robert Farquharson was driving when his car left the road and sank beneath the waters of a dam. He escaped from the sinking vehicle, but ten-year-old Jai, seven-year-old Tyler and two-year-old Bailey Farquharson all drowned.

Early next day police divers discovered the bodies of the boys...

Farquharson claimed that he had temporarily blacked out after suffering a coughing fit while driving, and that his out of control car then veered into the dam. He then reportedly dived below the water in an unsuccessful attempt to rescue his sons. The police called to the death scene became increasingly sceptical about Farquharson's explanation of the events that occurred.

They noted tyre marks that showed the car had proceeded directly through a fence and into the water, and there was no indication that the vehicle had veered in any way from its course. They also discovered that Farquharson had no

...the lights of the car had been turned off before the vehicle entered the water...

previous history of coughing attacks, and that he refused offers of help from bystanders, who volunteered to search for the boys in the water.

Later he stood by and watched while his ex-wife's new partner dived frequently under the waters of the dam, in an unsuccessful attempt to locate the boys. When help from others became available, he twice refused to ring emergency services. After clambering up the bank onto the highway roadside, he persuaded a motorist to drive eight kilometres to his estranged wife's house, so that he personally relayed the grim news about the triple fatalities.

Early next day police divers discovered the bodies of the boys, and the car was also dredged out of the dam. Investigators found that both the older children managed to release themselves from their car seats as the car sank, but that they perished before they could free Bailey from his harness. Police also discovered that the lights of the car had been turned off before the vehicle entered the water, and that the car was in good mechanical condition.

Two days after the tragedy occurred, Robert Farquharson was interviewed in his home by homicide detectives, and he was later charged with the murders of his three sons. At his trial expert

Rachel Pfitzner

opinions varied about the validity of Farquharson's coughing attack, but Gary King's recall of Farquharson's threats to his family were especially damaging. On November 17th 2007, he was sentenced to life imprisonment without parole.

His ex-wife, Cindy Gambino, has consistently supported his claims that he did not deliberately kill his three children.

"He would not harm a hair on their heads," she declared. "It was an accident... I don't believe that it was murder."

Farquharson's two sisters also continue to support their brother's claims of innocence.

...he had been shaken to death about ten days before his body was discovered in the pond.

A TRAGEDY WAITING TO HAPPEN

The body of two-year-old Dean Shillingsworth was found by children floating in a suitcase on a Sydney pond in June 2007. His mother, 26-year-old Rachel Pfitzner, had recently been released from custody, and the deceased toddler had been the focus of a custody battle between his grandparents in Tamworth and his mother in Sydney.

The boy disappeared after failing to return to Tamworth from an access visit with his mother. An examination of the child's body led police to believe that he had been shaken to death about ten days before his body was discovered in the pond. Next day Rachel Pfitzner was arrested and charged with murder.

Neighbours of the mother reported that she had an unhappy relationship with her estranged husband, but he was released without charge after being interviewed by police.

On 5 June 2009 Pfitzner pleaded guilty to manslaughter but not guilty to murder in front of the NSW Supreme Court. In August the same year, she revised her plea to guilty of murder and was later sentenced to 25 years 6 months in gaol.

CHAPTER FIVE:

WEIRD AND BIZARRE CASES

A PREMIER DENIED

Prior to 1961, Robert Peter Tait had a string of relatively minor convictions for unlawful wounding and offensive behaviour. He also spent two years in custody for assaulting and robbing a 70-year-old librarian.

The friendless, alcoholic deviant graduated to the extremely dangerous category, when he molested, assaulted and murdered 84-year-old Mrs Ada Hall, the mother of George Hall, who was a vicar in Hawthorn. Tait arrived at the vicarage on 8th August 1961, hoping that the Reverend Hall would provide him with financial assistance.

The elderly woman was the only person on the premises, and Tait savagely attacked her. After Mrs Hall lapsed into unconsciousness, he removed her underwear. Several other items of underwear were stolen from Ada Hall's bedroom drawer, and the obnoxious attacker dressed himself in some of these items of women's clothing.

Tait then fled from the premises, after stealing items of jewellery and money, and hitch-hiked to South Australia. There he was reported to police by a truck driver, who had been given a woman's brooch by Tait. When he was arrested in Port Augusta, Tait was found to be wearing Ada Hall's stolen underwear. He admitted to the vicarage murder, and was extradited to Melbourne.

...the obnoxious attacker dressed himself in items of women's clothing.

On 12th December 1961, Robert Peter Tait was found guilty of murder and sentenced to death, despite doubts already being expressed about his sanity. As the time of execution drew near in 1962, an emotional storm of protest broke out among many in the general public. However submissions to the Court of Criminal Appeals and the High Court were rejected, and the Victorian Executive Council declined to remit Tait's sentence. The then Victorian Premier, Mr. (later Sir Henry), Bolte staunchly supported the death sentence being enacted.

Legal battles regarding Tait's sanity continued to be waged, and Full Court judges complained that they were under increasing pressure to reach a quick verdict before the execution date. Two days before Tait's appointment with the hangman, the Chief Secretary was issued with an order of restraint from the Victorian Government, and Tait was reprieved only hours after his grave had been freshly dug in the grounds of Pentridge Prison.

On 5th November 1962, Premier Bolte announced that Tait had been certified insane, and his sentence was commuted to life imprisonment. By the middle of 1963 Tait's mental condition improved noticeably, and he was transferred from his psychiatric institution back to Pentridge where he died in 1984.

The death penalty in Victoria remained in place, and it is believed by some that Premier Bolte strongly supported Ronald Ryan paying the ultimate price for murder five years later, as a recompense for Tait's reprieve.

SCHOOL'S OUT

...woman teacher and all six students kidnapped by two armed men.

When Australians collected their morning papers on Saturday October 7th 1972, they were confronted by headline news so bizarre that it was almost unbelievable.

In the previous 24 hours, a small one-teacher school in Central Victoria, had its female teacher and all six students kidnapped by two armed men. A million dollars cash ransom was demanded for the safe release of the victims.

Police later speculated that Edwin John Eastwood and Robert Clyde Boland, were influenced to commit their outrageous crime, by a scene from the then recent movie "Dirty Harry". In the film, a bus load of school children are taken hostage, and the chilling real life drama that Eastwood and Boland enacted had disturbing similarities to the same theme.

All the hostages would be killed...

Eastwood and Boland entered the Faraday Primary School at about 3 pm on Friday, 6th October. The teacher, 20-year-old Mary Gibbs, and her six girl students aged between five and ten, were forced at gunpoint into a red delivery van. The kidnapped school group was then driven off into a remote area of bushland, after a ransom note was left behind in the classroom. The written message was starkly brutal: All the hostages would be killed unless a million dollars was paid for their safe release.

That evening the then Premier of Victoria, Rupert "Dick" Hamer, announced that the State Government was prepared to pay the ransom. The Victorian Education Minister, (and future Premier), Mr. Lindsay Thompson, arrived at the designated hand over site, and bravely waited alone to personally deliver the ransom money. It was never collected.

However in the early hours of next morning, the kidnappers told Mary Gibbs they were going to collect the ransom, and they left her and the frightened, bewildered children locked in the van near a bush track.

After the evil duo departed Ms Gibbs showed daring initiative and courage. Using her heavy platform-heeled leather boots, she kicked out a door panel of the van and escaped with the children into the dark bushland. Fortunately a search party found them a few kilometres away, so all the hostages were saved. On 2nd January 1973 after the ordeal was over, Mary Gibbs was awarded a George Medal for her bravery.

...the kidnappers planned to bury the school group alive...

Police later suspected that the kidnappers planned to bury the school group alive after they collected the lucrative ransom, but the available money was never collected, and both Boland and Eastwood were captured by police after an extensive manhunt.

Eastwood pleaded guilty at his 1972 trial, and was gaoled for 15 years. The legal process for Boland was more prolonged, but in 1974, at his third trial, he was sentenced to 16 years behind bars. Most believed they would never see such a weird crime replicated, but Edwin Eastwood maintained his bizarre fixation.

In December 1976, Eastwood escaped from Geelong Prison. He successfully evaded efforts to recapture him, and, to the amazement of all, on 15th February 1977, Edwin John Eastwood kidnapped a male teacher and nine students from the Wooreen

Primary school in Victoria's Gippsland area.

When he recklessly drove off with his victims, he collided with a truck, and Eastwood promptly added the truck driver and his passenger to his growing list of hostages. He then stole a campervan carrying three elderly women, who were also kidnapped.

He then stole a campervan carrying three elderly women...

By then the number of hostages had reached 15, and Eastwood announced his ambitious "wish list". For the safe release of his prisoners, the sum of $7,000,000 American dollars was demanded, along with a supply of drugs and guns, and the release of 17 inmates from Pentridge Prison.

One hostage fortunately escaped before authorities could act upon these ultimatums, and Eastwood fled from the scene. He was finally recaptured after his third stolen car ran out of petrol, but the desperate escapee received a gun shot in the right knee before he was forced to surrender.

The serial kidnapper later pleaded guilty to 25 charges that included kidnapping, conduct endangering life, escaping from legal custody and car theft, and received an additional 21 years in prison. As this sentence was cumulative with the ten years still to be served for the Faraday kidnapping, it effectively meant that Edwin Eastwood received a custodial sentence of 31 years. He was released from prison in 1993.

ONE BODY, TWO BURIALS

For almost 20 years Dennis Hunter's three daughters believed that their mother had abandoned the family, and run off with another man. In reality their father killed Verda Hunter in October 1981, by battering her with a piece of wood during one of their frequent violent arguments.

He then placed her body in a hole that he dug in the garden, before covering the shallow grave with wood, and setting the pyre on fire. Soon after, bricks were laid over the secret grave. Twelve years later Hunter dug up the body, and buried his dead wife again. This time the remains were deposited under the slab floor of a garage he was building.

Persistent doubts by Verda Hunter's brother about the circumstances behind his sister's disappearance from her Traralgon home, caused police to investigate further, and Dennis Hunter confessed to killing his wife 19 ½ years after she allegedly walked out of the marriage. He claimed that she was chasing him around the house with a knife on the night of her death, and that he killed her in self defence.

...chasing him around the house with a knife on the night of her death...

Dennis Hunter further alleged that Verda had frequently displayed dangerous behaviour for over a decade, and that she urgently needed professional psychiatric help. Their children loathed and feared their mother because she often beat them savagely, a claim that was supported by all his three children and a neighbour. Her workmates and others, however, remembered Verda Hunter as a shy and quiet person.

A second marriage for Hunter ended prematurely, when Vicki died of breast cancer. Her battle with the illness caused Hunter to take a redundancy payment from the SEC, (after 26 years of employment), so that he could care for her needs. Hunter also previously experienced tragedy with one of his children, as his son David died after being stabbed at St. Kilda Beach.

After Dennis Hunter's murder case came to court, Verda's brother admitted that she did exhibit reality problems in her daily life, and none of the defendant's three daughters testified against him. The 57-year-old Hunter was found guilty of manslaughter, and gaoled for seven years with a non-parole period of four years and six months. His ex brother-in-law was disgusted with the jury's decision, and claimed that Dennis Hunter's actions in secretly burying and burning the body of his sister, was not given due regard by the court.

...secretly burying and burning the body...

IN YOUR DREAMS BERNIE

On at least two occasions in the history of crime, accused men have successfully claimed that they were asleep when they killed others.

In 1846 in Boston USA, Albert Tirrell entered a brothel, slit the throat of a prostitute, and then lit three fires in the building. At his subsequent trial, Tirrell claimed that he was sleep walking when the acts were committed, and after two hours deliberation, a jury amazingly set him free.

...on at least 2 occasions accused men have successfully claimed that they were asleep when they killed others.

Another bizarre case occurred in Canada in 1987, which began after a man drove his car for 23 kilometres to his in-law's home. Soon after he arrived, he killed both of his relatives by marriage, but claimed that he was not responsible for his actions because he was asleep when the couple were slain. He was also found not guilty of murder.

Australia experienced its own "sleep walking" homicide case on 26th August 1992. For many years before the fatality, Bernie Brown had an extraordinary history of sleep walking, which began in his childhood day at a Western Australian orphanage. There on waking, he would often find himself lying on a shelf, well away from his bed. His condition appeared to improve, until a heavy knock to the head in 1988 appeared to reactivate the tendency.

...he awoke one morning, the bloodied body of his wife of ten years lay near him...

By August 1992, Bernie Brown feared that his ongoing employment as a house painter was in doubt, and during that stressful time he started waking up away from his bedroom in other parts of the house. Late that same month, when he awoke one morning in his own bed, the bloodied body of his wife of ten years lay near him on the floor. Susan Brown had been struck with a claw hammer, and shot twice in the back of the head.

The husband removed the sheets and other stained items in the room, and hid them in his car. He then wiped further blood spots from the wall, and cleaned himself thoroughly in the shower, before waking his sleeping children. They were informed that their mother was not well, and that he would stay home from work to care for her. In this typical domestic scenario, Brown's behaviour was normal, and the children made their way happily to school after being provided with money for their lunches.

The façade of calmness vanished by 9.30 am however, when a distraught Brown confessed to a friend. Police were soon contacted, and 30 minutes later Brown claimed in an interview situation that he had no idea how his wife's life violently ended.

At his first trial, Bernard Brown was found guilty of knowingly murdering his wife, but the case was far from over. In December 1993 a Queensland Court of Appeals overturned that decision. Then on 4th January 1995, just before the commencement of a second trial, a sensational new development occurred. Brown changed his plea to guilty, and he subsequently received a life imprisonment sentence.

It is still open to debate about what the final outcome would have been in this bizarre case, if Bernard Brown had not finally confessed to committing the murder.

A FAILED MIRACLE

One of the saddest and most bizarre homicide cases in Victoria's history occurred in the summer of 1993 at Antwerp, a tiny hamlet in the Wimmera area of the state.

The family at the centre of the tragedy were the Vollmers, who operated a small pig farm. On 23rd January, 54-year-old Ralph Vollmer observed his wife wildly dancing and yelling outside their house. She had previously been institutionalised for schizophrenia. In more recent times, however, the couple had addressed her problems by regularly attending prayer meetings conducted by a small charismatic religious group. Ralph sought the advice of his nearby neighbours who were local leaders of the cult. Leanne and

...observed his wife wildly dancing and yelling outside their house.

John Reichenberg gravely informed the concerned husband that his wife was possessed by the devil, and that exorcism was the only remedy.

Hours of prayer followed for the trio, while the agitated woman was forcibly restrained. Then, on or around 28th January, two more cult members arrived to assist in the "cleansing" process.

By then Mrs Vollmer was allegedly possessed by ten demons...

By then Mrs Vollmer was allegedly possessed by ten demons, which included "the spirit of filth, abuse and legion", a particularly strong force which they believed possessed the strength of 2,000 normal people. At this stage of the "treatment", Mrs Vollmer was displaying abnormal strength in the oppressively hot conditions, and had swelled up as though she were pregnant.

On 30th January further help arrived from Melbourne in the form of Matthew Nuske, a 22-year-old greenkeeper and secret exorcist. He ran pieces of cling-wrap seven times around the Vollmer house, while the group prayed and commanded the evil forces to expel themselves from the victim's body.

By then they believed the alleged demons were located in the woman's womb, and they endeavoured to vigorously force them from her stomach, throat and mouth. However by the end of the month "terrible hissing sounds were coming out of her mouth, and the lights went out of her eyes when the demons came out". By February 1st the group realised that the unfortunate woman was dead, and the police were finally contacted. When officers arrived at the scene the swollen, decomposing body had almost liquefied in the oppressively hot conditions. As far as they could ascertain, the woman had died after suffering severe internal injuries.

"I know this will happen... the whole thing is God's plan. Before her body is lowered into the grave, He is going to raise her up again..."

The devout fundamentalist group allegedly delayed informing police about the fatality, because "phone calls from people very sensitive to the Lord" had told them the deceased victim would soon "rise from the dead". No one was more adamant about the coming miracle than Ralph Vollmer.

"I do not (only) believe; I know this will happen," he informed TV reporters and other media outlets. "The whole thing is God's plan. Before her body is lowered into the grave, He is going to raise her up again, and I hope and pray that your cameras will be there, because the Lord wants the world to see this."

Only hours before the burial service began, Ralph confided that he had received further "promises" in regard to his wife's resurrection, and about 30 reporters and photographers, together with scores of mourners and other curious bystanders, gathered to witness the promised miracle.

The actual outcome was shattering for Ralph Vollmer. After the coffin was lowered into the grave, and the resurrection failed to eventuate, he collapsed in disbelief. Later he, and others in the fundamentalist group, rationalised that Mrs Vollmers did not return to this world at the funeral service because she was too fond of her new heavenly home.

...the resurrection failed to eventuate, he collapsed in disbelief.

Ralph Vollmer and Matthew Nuske were found guilty of unlawful imprisonment, while Leanne Reichenberg and David Klingner were convicted of manslaughter.

It proved impossible for pathologists to determine the exact causes of death by the time they examined the badly decomposed body. Consequently magistrate Tim McDonald dismissed all charges against the accused because of insufficient evidence.

ALREADY DEAD

The 41-year-old disabled man died on a walk in the Victorian town of Ararat. Shortly before his demise, he had been searching for pink golf balls for his twin sister Judith Anne Cenzic, with whom he had spent five happy hours on an early May day in 1994.

Lindsay Jellett had been brain damaged since the age of two, after a car crashed into his pram. His life since then had depended on much family support, but Lindsay's situation had improved in recent times. He had moved from institutionalised care at Aradale, to a residential home in the town. His epilepsy was now well controlled by medication, and he was the recipient of $105,000 in compensation. On that particular visit, his sister had spent $55 on pursuits he enjoyed, such as "playing the pokies".

Concerns were felt for Jellett when he disappeared soon after Cenzic departed at 4 pm, and later that day his body was found on the side of the road. The injuries he sustained suggested that he had been deliberately run over by a car, and police soon suspected that Judith Cenzic was the culprit.

Greed was considered to be Cenzic's motive as she stood to inherit much of her brother's compensation money. Her usual two hour trip back to Melton had taken over four hours on 10th May, and police believed that she had returned to Ararat shortly after she first left, and deliberately reversed the car over her unsuspecting brother. A witness later claimed that he saw a car similar to Cenzic's near the crime scene, well after her apparent departure at 4 pm.

...deliberately reversed the car over her unsuspecting brother.

The accused claimed that she visited a car wash establishment on her journey home, and she was further delayed by picking up her youngest two children from another residence. Cenzic also voiced the possibility that her car had been stolen from her driveway, and later returned after the perpetrator killed her brother. Her older adult son, Greg, cast doubts on the alibis, but he may have had a hostile agenda towards his mother. She had recently refused to help finance the purchase of a car for his use.

Evidence against Cenzic continued to mount, and when investigators established a Lindsay Jellett DNA link to human blood, fabric and samples of hair found on the underside of his sister's car, an arrest was imminent.

A pathologist connected with the case then unexpectedly added a bizarre twist, when he revealed that Lindsay Jellett was actually dead before the car reversed over him.

...killing a corpse is an impossible act.

Judith Cenzic was still charged with deliberately suffocating and then deliberately driving over Lindsay Jellett, despite submissions that Jellett possibly died from an epilepsy attack. In court, Justice Tom Smith ordered the jury to acquit Cenzic of the charge of murder, because killing a corpse is an impossible act. He added, however, that a verdict of attempted murder could be considered.

On 26th July 1996, a jury found Judith Anne Cenzic guilty of attempted murder, and the judge sentenced the thrice married woman and mother of three children, to ten years in custody with a minimum of six. Cenzic stressed that she had previously rejected opportunities to control her brother's money in her plea of innocence. Her efforts failed, because in June 1997 an appeal against her sentence was refused.

PLAYGROUND HORROR

It was a typical school playground scene on 10th October 1996, with laughing children happily playing together. Then, at 1.40 pm at this Cairns Primary School, the life of an innocent six-year-old boy changed drastically when a young adult male suddenly appeared among the group of children. He poured petrol over an unsuspecting Tjandamurra O'Shane and set him on fire, while his schoolmates watched in horror. The stranger then casually strolled away from the disaster, and surrendered himself to a traffic policeman outside the school.

He poured petrol over an unsuspecting Tjandamurra O'Shane and set him on fire...

The school principal was close at hand when the attack occurred, and he continually rolled the boy over in the dirt to douse the flames. He suffered burns to his own hands and leg, but his quick, brave reaction probably saved the boy's life.

Tjandamurra O'Shane, the nephew of Judge

"I wanted to punish people for ruining my life."

Pat O'Shane, the first aboriginal magistrate in Australia, then began a long and traumatic fight to recovery. He suffered burns to 75% of his body, and for some time remained in a critical condition in the Brisbane Royal Children's Hospital. Several major skin grafts were necessary, and the boy was unable to speak for some time because of tubes being inserted down his throat.

For over six weeks he remained heavily bandaged in an infection controlled room, and after he was released from hospital in the early months of 1997, Tjandamurra O'Shane had to wear a restrictive pressure suit for another two years. The nation warmed to the little boy's heroism, with many people generously donating money to assist his rehabilitation.

It is difficult to provide a rational explanation for the perpetrator's monstrously cruel act. Twenty-seven-year-old Paul Wade Streeton had only resided in Cairns for a week before he randomly attacked O'Shane, and police did not consider the act was politically or racially motivated. The unemployed South Australian social worker, provided this bitter and self-indulgent reason for committing his heinous crime.

"I wanted to punish people for ruining my life." He added that his parents and educational authorities had failed to recognise his intelligence, that he had been planning such an attack since his Year Two school days, and that he did not wish to continue living. He added that there was nothing personal in his attack on the boy, and that he hoped to receive the death sentence for his crime. He admitted to the crime of causing grievous bodily harm, but denied he was guilty of attempted murder.

At his trial in March 1997, Justice Margaret White was unimpressed by Streeton's plea, and accurately described him as being "a bitter, selfish and self-centred person". He was given a life sentence without parole, which is only the third time in Australian history that a crime other than murder has received such a severe penalty. It has since been reported that Paul Wade Streeton has been moved into protective custody, because of constant threats to his life from other prison inmates.

THE WORLD'S WORST HITMAN

...wanted her to become involved in couple swapping orgies.

Carmela Thessi was seriously "under whelmed" by her overweight 41-year-old husband John, who wanted her to become involved in couple swapping orgies. In 1994 the annoyed woman contacted a former workmate in Suzette Glassby, and allegedly informed her that $30,000-

$50,000 was available for the contract killing of her husband.

It proved to be an irresistible offer for the four-month-pregnant heroin addict. At that time, she and her also drug-addicted husband Gary, were living in poor circumstances on an invalid pension in a Sydney caravan park. The former prostitute first met her future husband at a methadone clinic they were both attending.

The incompetent marksman missed with his first shot at point blank range...

Gary Glassby's background in crime was both violent and unsuccessful. He had supposedly torched the home of an ex-girlfriend's mother, and after being acquitted of that offence, he murdered a fellow prisoner at Goulburn gaol in 1987.

Glassby posed as a dating agent contact, whose wife was allegedly willing to have sex with John Thessi. The amorous man readily agreed to a meeting, and Glassby drove Thessi towards the alleged rendezvous, with Suzette secretly trailing them in another vehicle.

The journey ended abruptly when Glassby produced a gun and forced the now terrified man to kneel on the ground near the parked car. The incompetent marksman missed with his first shot at point blank range, and the murder attempt was further stalled when the gun jammed. After two more attempts the execution was finally completed.

Investigators soon found evidence that implicated the couple. Written details of the planned homicide were found in Gary Glassby's pocket, and witnesses came forward who had seen Carmela and him in deep conversation. Listening devices in the Glassby's caravan home provided further damning proof, and on 11th November 1997 the husband was sentenced to life imprisonment, while his wife was placed in custody for nine months.

The case against Carmela Thessi, who allegedly planned the execution of her husband, was not proceeded with because of the lack of credible evidence.

BEYOND BELIEF

Breatharians maintain that they can be fed by the light of God, so for the true believers normal food is deemed unnecessary. They believe that they breathe God, and derive their nourishment from "liquid light", which is reputedly a universal form of electricity that removes the need for food or drink. The process is not a miracle, but a sacred, spiritual journey which reclaims a natural state of being.

Breatharians maintain that they can be fed by the light of God, so for the true believers normal food is deemed unnecessary.

These beliefs were advanced by Jasmuheen, the Australian breatharian "guru" in her book "Living on Light". In 1983 Wiley Brooks, the

Jasmuheen

American founder of the movement, was reportedly seen slinking out of a 7-Eleven store with a slurpee, a hot dog and twinkies for sustenance, which produced wry smiles from many sceptics of the movement. Back in Australia, Lani Morris remained a true believer.

She had produced nine children in her 30 year marriage, one of whom she later re-named Jasmuheen after her spiritual hero. However, following the death of her 23-year-old son, Lani abandoned her family and flew from Melbourne to Brisbane to be inducted into the movement. She was charged $700 for her 21-day course, and Jim and Eugenia Pesnak were the couple who volunteered to provide assistance for this controversial life change.

Sixty-year-old Jim Pesnak was a retired engineer while his 61-year-old wife Eugenia was a former tax agent. They had been breatharian followers for three years, though none of their four children shared their beliefs.

She would be required to have no food or drink for seven days...

Lani Morris domiciled herself in a caravan at the back of their home, and was briefed in the requirements of her course. She would be required to have no food or drink for seven days, and the process would then continue with a fortnight's diet of orange juice and other liquids.

The diary she kept in the caravan after commencing the course, indicated that Lani Morris was soon feeling ill and experiencing hallucinations. On the sixth day of her treatment, she was fully dressed when she had a shower, and at 4 pm that day the Pesnaks heard a thud from the caravan. Ms Morris had collapsed on the floor, and she had to be assisted back to her bed.

Finally she was allowed two litres of orange juice, but she was still physically weak, and her body functions were breaking down. Dr William Moulton, a medico, who then supported the breatharian philosophy, assured the Pesnaks in a phone conversation that the symptoms they described were a sign of Lani Morris' spiritual struggle to rid her body of poisons. Jim Pesnak later stated that the patient was then fighting an "ego battle with her emotional burdens".

...the symptoms they described were a sign of Lani Morris' spiritual struggle to rid her body of poisons.

By Monday 26th June 1999, Lani Morris was unable to speak, and Pesnak later recalled that "black stuff was coming out of her mouth". Milk diluted with warm water was provided for her, but an ambulance was still not called for two further days.

The now unconscious woman, whose lungs had ceased to function effectively, was taken to hospital where she died a week later. An examining neuro-pathologist believes that the patient might have survived, if an ambulance had been called a day earlier.

In November 1999, the Pesnaks faced charges of criminal negligence and manslaughter in the Brisbane Supreme Court. Their defence lawyers claimed that they were not guilty of a criminal offence, as they could not be convicted for their beliefs. The presiding judge compared their situation to the Vollmer case in Victoria, but after three hours deliberation the jury found the couple guilty of manslaughter. At first Jim and Eugenia Pesnak were sentenced to six and three year jail terms respectively, but the sentences were later effectively reduced to 18 months for the husband, and nine months for his wife.

While the Lani Morris drama came to its tragic conclusion, the Australian "guru" Jasmuheen distanced herself from the controversy. She stated that she knew none of the people involved, and "implored people to act responsibly at all times". Jasmuheen, formerly known as Ellen Greve, had her credibility as a breatharian leader tarnished, when it was revealed that the refrigerator at her own home was full of food. She claimed, however, that the food was only for the sustenance of Jess Ferguson, her second husband.

...challenge to personally demonstrate the credibility of breatharian practices.

A month before the Pesnak's trial began Jasmuheen accepted a Channel 9 "60 Minutes" challenge to personally demonstrate the credibility of breatharian practices. After four days the experiment was abandoned on the advice of Australian Medical Association (AMA) observers. Jasmuheen blamed her failure to continue the experiment on sleeplessness caused by media pressure, and pollution from a nearby freeway.

Jasmuheen finally gained public recognition when she received the 2000 Australian Sceptics Bent Spoon Award, for being the "perpetrator of the most preposterous piece of paranormal or pseudoscientific piffle" for the year.

"perpetrator of the most preposterous piece of paranormal or pseudoscientific piffle"

It was all a bit hard to swallow, and would have been a real hoot, except that a vulnerable woman died because she adopted the breatharian's bizarre practices.

MISGUIDED CHIVALRY

Twenty-seven-year-old John Edward Whiteside, and his 28-year-old companion Kristian Peter Dieber, did not appear to be modern day "Galahads" when they wended their way out of the Melbourne Cricket Ground (MCG) after the annual Anzac Day football match in 1999.

They were more typical of many football supporters; a couple of single men who enjoyed a day's barracking and drinking while they watched a closely contested sporting contest. The end of the day for them was drawing to a happy if somewhat hazy conclusion, when the two "knights in shining armour" were confronted by a "lady in distress" near Melbourne's Treasury Gardens.

"Are you going to rape me too?" wailed the weeping, hysterical woman. She then dramatically threw her wallet at the startled men, yelling "just take it and leave me alone" when the concerned two hurried towards her.

Whiteside and Dieber attempted to comfort her, and started to search for a taxi. She again declared that she had been sexually assaulted, and a passing jogger informed the now shocked and indignant duo, that he had just observed two men arguing with a woman in the park.

...in search of two men who they believed had raped the young woman.

A senior park ranger then appeared, and he was suspicious about the woman's claims when she became evasive in her replies to questions. The two now vengeful young men, aided by rush of testosterone that was well fuelled by alcohol, harboured no doubts about the validity of the distressed woman's claims. They stalked off angrily through the park in search of two men who they believed had raped the young woman.

Two hapless males were soon spotted. They were Keith Hibbins and David Campbell, a homosexual couple who had been involved in a secure relationship for 15 years. They were wary of "poofta" bashers in Melbourne's parklands, and when they were challenged by the two "vigilantes", the partially physically handicapped Hibbins panicked, and made the fatal decision to flee from the scene.

Tragically the young attackers' "noble mission" was all for nothing, as no rape had occurred.

Campbell was physically assaulted first, and the slow moving Hibbins was then easily caught, and brutally bashed and kicked into unconsciousness. Eleven days later 45-year-old Keith Hibbins died in hospital from his injuries, and two shocked young men were charged by police. A man had been assaulted, and his equally innocent gay companion killed. Tragically the young attackers' "noble mission" was all for nothing, as no rape had occurred.

On that fateful Anzac Day, Eugenia "Jenny" Tsionis was not a "lady in distress". As usual she was "off her face", with a potent mixture of drugs and alcohol. The former table top dancer had been on a day long binge with her boyfriend, Tony Beck. Substance abuse had commenced with a bong of marijuana for breakfast, followed by four glasses of spirits at the St Kilda Esplanade Hotel, and a steady supply of drinks for the remainder of the day.

Their binge took the pair into the city, and while driving through Melbourne's CBD district they began a fierce argument. Tsionis forced Beck

...the "lady in distress" accepted no responsibility for the tragedy caused by her lies.

to stop the car, and she angrily threw a shoe at him, before storming into Treasury Gardens, where she told her monstrous lie to the city's two unluckiest football supporters.

A month later she admitted that her rape story was false, but her retraction was of no benefit to Whiteside or Dieber. The pair were finally sentenced to six years gaol with a minimum of four for the assault of David Campbell and the fatal bashing of Keith Hibbins.

Finally each only served the pre-sentenced detention penalty of six months in custody.

And the "lady in distress" who was the catalyst of the whole thuggish incident? She accepted no responsibility for the tragedy caused by her lies.

On 15th October 1999, at the men's murder trial, an unrepentant "Jenny" Tsionis exonerated herself from any blame saying "I didn't tell them to do that (bash the victims)... It didn't give them the right to do that."

Tsionis received a two months intensive corrections order, after being found guilty of possessing a prohibited drug and providing a false report to police.

Justice sometimes moves in strange ways.

ROLE PLAY TRAGEDY

Peter Richard Barnwell was completely engrossed by the violent Robert de Niro video he watched at Luke O'Keefe's flat. After the movie finished, the 24-year-old found O'Keefe's gun, and he began to act out some of the graphic scenes he had just witnessed on the video. While he fantasised, he unintentionally fired a shot through the couch where his 25-year-old friend was sleeping and accidentally killed him.

...he began to act out some of the graphic scenes he had just witnessed on the video.

Barnwell had a troubled past well before the tragedy occurred. The South African emigrated from Durban with his family at the age of two, and he struggled both academically and socially during his school years in Australia. By the time he reached adulthood, he had a history of depression, petty crime and drug dependency.

Barnwell panicked when he realised that O'Keefe was dead. He fled from the flat and hid the gun. Then, after consuming a couple of stiff drinks, he dialled 000 and confessed his crime from a nearby Port Melbourne hotel.

On 5th July 2002, Barnwell was sentenced to four years' imprisonment with a minimum period of two years after pleading guilty to the charge of reckless manslaughter.

CHAPTER SIX:

REVENGE KILLINGS

CORRUPTION SUSPECTED IN UNSOLVED MURDER CASE

For years leading Western Australian politicians and policemen of the 1970s, have been suspected of being closely linked to the still unsolved 1975 murder of Shirley Finn. The "Queen of Vice", as Finn was then dubbed, was a wealthy Perth brothel madam, who lavishly entertained many "friends in high places" in her opulent heyday.

There were many potential problems in Finn's controversial lifestyle. At the time of her death, the 34-year-old mother of three was involved in a relationship with 25-year-old Rosalie Dean. She had recently repaid a debt of $1,000 to her father, and still owed the Taxation Department a hefty $100,000. In many ways it came as no surprise when she was discovered slumped in her car around 2am on 23rd

Shirley Finn

June, with fatal bullet wounds to her head.

Theories about her death included the notion that she was executed by other brothel owners who hired a contract killer, and there were also suspects from the outwardly respectable "big end of town". Investigations resulted in the Public Service Board sacking one of their lawyers who had alleged links to an escort agency. A senior member of the Criminal Investigation Bureau (CIB) was also questioned at length before being cleared. State premier Sir Charles Court offered a $20,000 reward for any information that would lead to a conviction in this much publicised case.

...damaging proof about bribes paid to senior police members...

Susan Deveneaux, another brothel owner, publicly expressed her belief that Shirley Finn was murdered because she was about to provide the Taxation Office with damaging proof about bribes paid to senior police members, to keep her brothel operational.

The unsolved case gained further momentum in September 1994, when the West Australian" newspaper attempted to gain vital evidence under Freedom of Information laws. It was then discovered that over half of the relevant documents were missing. Deputy Commissioner Les Ayton claimed that this serious discrepancy was caused by "a clerical error", which only led to more speculation.

After allegations were made that prominent Members of Parliament (MPs) made regular visits to Finn's brothel premises, publicity about the unsolved case increased, and a previously unknown source of information was revealed.

A man claimed that when Finn was murdered, he and his then girlfriend were parked in his car not far from where the crime took place. Shortly after hearing shots a torch was shone into his car, and two men in police uniforms, that carried no badge numbers, ordered the couple to move away immediately.

Since then rumours about the involvement of police and parliamentary representatives in graft, corruption, prostitution and the actual murder of Shirley Finn, have persisted to this day, but the identity of her killer or killers remains a mystery.

SHE KNEW TOO MUCH

Sallie Anne Huckstepp was a 32-year-old prostitute and drug user with friends and enemies from both the underworld and the NSW police department. Her fully clothed body was found in Sydney's Centennial Park on 7th February 1986.

...an autopsy revealed that she had been partly strangled before she drowned...

At first the case was treated as a suspicious death rather than murder. However an autopsy revealed that she had been partly strangled before

Sallie Anne Huckstepp

she drowned.

Sallie Anne Huckstepp was raised by her father and older sister Debra, and attended a Jewish private school. After leaving school, she became a heroin user and prostitute before being wed at the age of 17. Her husband was Bryan Huckstepp, a small time criminal. Her work as a prostitute continued, and the marriage produced a daughter named Sascha before the couple went their separate ways.

She then became involved in a relationship with a criminal called Warren Lanfranchi, and fell pregnant again. Lanfranchi had stolen $37,000 worth of drugs from a dealer who had close links with Ralph Rogerson, a corrupt police detective. A meeting to sort out this problem was arranged between Rogerson and Lanfranchi. Repayment arrangements were to be discussed, and it is also rumoured that Lanfranchi was expected to pay a further $50,000, in order to have an attempted murder charge dropped.

...she became a heroin user and prostitute before being wed at the age of 17.

Rogerson and three other detectives were allegedly going to arrest Lanfranchi at the designated meeting place, and it was at this location that the criminal was shot dead. The police group claimed that Lanfranchi was gunned down by Rogerson with two shots from his Smith and Weston .38 calibre revolver after the criminal first aimed a silver revolver at Rogerson. It was later found that Lanfranchi's gun was a one shot defective weapon.

No money was found in Lanfranchi's clothes, yet Sallie Anne Huckstepp later claimed on the TV program "60 Minutes" that her lover had $10,000 with him to pay to Rogerson. An official inquiry was called, but the only non-police witness was the notorious criminal, Neddy Smith. Coroner Walsh found that no indictable offence could be revealed from the available evidence. He also suggested to the jury that they might consider bravery recommendations for the actions taken by the police group, but this opportunity was not taken up.

A traumatised Sally-Anne lost her child in a miscarriage, and soon after she began a new career as a freelance writer for "Penthouse". However before long she began using and dealing heroin again, and after a friend died of an overdose, Sally Anne confided her belief that her own life was in danger, from both police and underworld figures. She sent her daughter Sascha to live with her father, before her body was found in early 1986.

...she began a new career as a freelance writer for "Penthouse".

An inquest lasting over four years into Sallie Anne Huckstepp's death began in 1987. During this long process, many false claims were made by various heroin addicts and criminals in taped conversations, but finally Coroner Glass pro-

...her sister died because "she knew too much".

duced his conclusions in February 1991.

Glass found that Sallie Anne Huckstepp had been murdered by a person or persons unknown. The NSW government offered a reward of $50,000 for information that resulted in an arrest, and the deceased's sister Debra claimed that her sister died because "she knew too much".

In September 1996 magistrate Pat O'Shane found that there was sufficient evidence to charge Neddy Smith with Huckstepp's murder. By then the hardened criminal was suffering chronically from Parkinson's disease, but was expected to face a future trial.

A KILLER OR AN INNOCENT "NUTTER"?

In the early evening of 10th January 1989, the then Assistant Commissioner of Federal police died after receiving two bullet wounds to the head in the driveway of his Canberra home. The weapon used to kill Colin Winchester was a .22 calibre self-loading Ruger rifle, which police claimed was either fired by a professional killer or an amateur riding his luck. Nearby residents recall hearing a V8 type engine vehicle rapidly leaving the area, around the time of the shooting.

First theories centred on organised crime

identities. Within 24 hours of the shooting, Australian Federal Police (AFP) officers were notified by an anonymous source that the murder related to a local drug syndicate. Winchester was due to provide evidence that would expose corrupt police personnel. The caller also provided well informed information about a situation that was not widely known.

Later Commander Bob McDonald, the head of the NSW branch of the AFP, produced a report that referred to an alleged Canberra meeting between two policemen and Italian criminals prior to Winchester's murder. A Ukrainian hitman called Jabranov was allegedly hired from overseas to perform the execution. Lennie McPherson and George Freeman, two notorious Sydney gangsters, were also persons of interest in the McDonald report, which was later rejected by the AFP.

Winchester was due to provide evidence that would expose corrupt police personnel.

Three years rolled by without any arrests being made until, to the disbelief of many, 44-year-old David Harold Eastman was charged with murdering Winchester. The myopic and extremely neurotic former public servant had been a prime suspect from the time investigations began, and circumstantial evidence against him was compelling.

A month before the shooting Eastman had a heated argument with Winchester about what

"He (Winchester) was the first man I ever killed. It was a beautiful thing, one of the most beautiful feelings I've ever known."

Eastman claimed was an unfair assault charge. On that occasion he uttered death threats against Winchester, and police claim that Eastman later stated

"He (Winchester) was the first man I ever killed. It was a beautiful thing, one of the most beautiful feelings I've ever known."

Eastman formerly owned the same type of weapon that was used in the murder. Furthermore he was identified as being at the home of a man who sold that type of weapon, and gunshot residue found in Eastman's car matched samples later found at the crime scene.

Only 18 hours after the homicide occurred Eastman was interviewed, but he was unable to recall his movements on the night of the murder. The suspect had a history of mental illness, and later a psychiatric report questioned whether David Eastman was fit to face trial. The report highlighted Eastman's long history of paranoia, and his complete inability to exert any self control.

Many locals were well aware of the suspect's uncontrollable temper. Five years before Eastman was arrested in 1992, he was charged with assaulting his neighbour. A psychiatrist then described him as having "a typically dangerous paranoid personality." In total, he was the recipient of 90 minor offences which included trying to push a fellow bushwalker's head into a camp fire. He had also been expelled from various hotels. His youth hostel and Australian Labor Party memberships had been cancelled.

Legal proceedings against the accused began in 1995, and the worst of David Eastman's many enemies could not have scripted a more disastrous approach to courtroom tactics. Eastman verbally abused a presiding judge, and in the first six months he sacked four legal teams. When he ill-advisedly conducted his own defence, Eastman only investigated two Crown witnesses. In the 70th day of a marathon 87-day trial, he declared that he would not even address the jury before it passed judgement on him. A change of mind saw Eastman's legal team return, but he was found guilty.

Eastman verbally abused a presiding judge, and in the first six months he sacked four legal teams.

Eastman continued to be his own worst enemy. During High Court Appeals in June 1999 and March 2000, he sacked both of his legal teams. This drastic step badly negated telling new evidence put forward by the late Colin Winchester's former neighbour. She claimed that on the night in question she saw two people near the Assistant Commissioner's residence. One of them resembled a well known drug trafficker who owned a V8 engine vehicle.

David Eastman, whose mental condition noticeably deteriorated before he was 30, was found guilty of murdering Colin Winchester and gaoled for life. In 2016, the ACT government announced that they were seeking a retrial of David Eastman, believing that there had been a miscarriage of justice in his case. In 2018, Eastman was found not guilty and was awarded just over $7 million in compensation.

SINS OF THE FATHER?

In June 1991, the body of Nancy King was found face down in a water filled pit on her Tallygaroopna farm near Shepparton in Victoria. Sixteen years later, her husband Graeme King was charged with her murder.

...the body of Nancy King was found face down in a water filled pit...

Jason King, the son of the accused man, had little affection for his father, and he was never satisfied about the circumstances surrounding his mother's death. Three days before she died, Nancy King informed him that she wished to leave his father, and that a $60,000 insurance payout would assist her in becoming financially independent.

Soon after her body was found, Jason King was shocked when he read a solicitor's letter which urged Graeme King to organise an inquest as soon as possible, so that he would quickly become the beneficiary of the insurance policy.

After Jason King confided his misgivings to local police, they advised him to secretly tape record any conversations with his father that pertained to Nancy King's death.

When the woman's body was first discovered, police believed that there was insufficient evidence to charge Graeme King with her murder. Shelley Robertson, the coroner assigned to the case then, was surprised by this decision, and years later she welcomed the reopening of the case.

...were still troubled about the bruises and abrasions that were evident then on the drowned corpse.

She and others were still troubled about the bruises and abrasions that were evident then on the drowned corpse. Other significant circumstantial evidence resurfaced in 2005, when the homicide squad re-opened this "cold" case.

At the time of Nancy King's death, Graeme King was involved in a sexual relationship with a local female cattle breeder. The affair continued for months after the wife died, before King's mistress ended the liaison due to his heavy drinking and her own concerns about the circumstances of Nancy King's death.

It was also revealed that King was deeply in debt before the insurance payment materialised, and during her marriage to the former local football identity, Nancy King frequently suffered both physical and emotional abuse. It was also unusual that no mud was found on the wife's gumboots, as the ground around the tank area was soggy.

King's four children, as well as his own four brothers and many other acquaintances, never believed that Nancy King's death was accidental, and at the 2007 hearing new evidence from an exotic dancer proved to be illuminating.

Susan Molnar was a table top dancer at Shepparton's Club Rawhide, when she met Graeme King at her place of work in 2000. During a conversation with him, she expressed sorrow about his wife's death, and allegedly received this startling reply.

"Don't be (sorry). I hated her. I killed her."

"Don't be (sorry). I hated her. I killed her."

Ms Molnar related the essence of that conversation to a male workmate that same night, but King denied making that comment. He claimed that he loved his wife, and that he did not murder her. In December 2007 a retrial was ordered after the jury failed to reach a unanimous verdict. In 2008, Graeme King was acquitted by the Victorian Supreme Court.

CENTRAL COAST SLAUGHTER

Around mid-October in 2002, 43-year-old Malcolm George Baker had an arsenal of weapons confiscated by police. This action was part of a restraining order condition that was taken out by his 23-year-old de facto partner of seven years, Kerryann Gannon. Baker, however, hid a shotgun at a location 24 kilometres away, and this action later resulted in fatal consequences on a massive scale.

...confessed that he had murdered six people with his shotgun.

On 28th October, the unemployed labourer surrendered himself to police at the Toukley station, and confessed that he had murdered six people with his shotgun.

Revenge was the principal reason for the calculated slaughter. The killings started in the NSW central coast town of Terrigal, where he shot down his ex-de facto partner, her heavily pregnant 18-year-old sister Lisa, and their father Thomas Gannon. Baker later blamed him for most of his domestic problems. Kerryann's new boyfriend Chris Gall was also shot, but he survived the murderous assault.

The killing spree then moved ten kilometres away to Bateau Bay, where Baker fatally wounded his 27-year-old son David, whom he claimed had intercourse with Kerryann, and provided her with drugs.

The gunman then moved on to nearby North Wyong where he targeted 35-year-old Ross Smith who allegedly owed Baker money. Smith and his unlucky 25-year-old visitor, Leslie Read, who was a stranger to Baker, were both shot dead.

In August 1993, Malcolm George Baker pleaded guilty to six counts of murder and one of attempted murder. Justice Newman sentenced him to penal servitude for life, with no prospect of parole.

UPDATE ON MISTAKEN IDENTITY MURDER

Early clues suggested that it was a tragic case of mistaken identity...

In November 1997 Melbournians grieved for Jane Thurgood-Dove after she was gunned down in her Niddrie driveway by an unknown assailant. Early clues suggested that it was a tragic case of mistaken identity, and that the real target of the execution was Carmel Kyprie.

There were both stark differences and uncanny similarities about the Thurgood-Dove and Kyprie families. Mark and Jane Thurgood-Dove were law abiding citizens who had no known enemies, whereas Peter Kyprie was a career criminal who was hated by many. Just three years before the Muriel Street murder, police had aborted a criminal plot to kill Peter Kyprie.

Both families had four wheel drive vehicles, they each had school age children and the two wives had similar hairstyles. The Kypries and the Thurgood-Doves both resided in Muriel Street, and their respective houses were located three from a corner.

However there were two corners in Niddrie's Muriel Street, because two different roads intersected in the street. Perhaps it was small details like this which confused the contract killers, and resulted in an innocent wife and mother being gunned down in front of her own children.

Jane Thurgood-Dove

Noted crime writer John Silvester believes that "hitmen", (those who accept contracts to kill others), are not usually well organised and clear thinking professionals. Often they are low life characters who are too lazy to work, too stupid to plan major crimes and too immoral to ask any searching questions of themselves. This "curriculum vitae" fitted the two Niddrie executors like a glove, but by the time police knew their identities, it was impossible to convict them.

...chased the frightened woman around her vehicle before gunning her down

Both contract killers are dead. Steven Mordy, the 40-year-old pot bellied gunman who chased the frightened woman around her vehicle before gunning her down, was a former Rebels bike gang member. For 18 months after the slaying, the Geelong resident lived like a recluse before dying of an overdose and related health problems in September 2001. Mordy had a violent past and was a previous suspect in a murder case.

His friend Jamie Reynolds was Mordy's driver on that fateful 1997 day. He allegedly admitted to a friend a week after the murder that "we got the wrong sheila". Reynolds subsequently chose the wrong day to go sailing, for he perished in a boat off Barwon Heads in April 2004. It was rumoured that the pair were offered $20,000 for the Muriel Street contract, but no money changed hands after the wrong target was eliminated.

Police know then who pulled the trigger, but who ordered the "hit"?

The prime suspect appears to be Phillip Peters, an allegedly corrupt lawyer who is sometimes called "Mr. Laundry", because of his reported ability to "wash" dirty money for criminals. Peters is apparently not very capable in schemes that require elementary attention to detail.

Sheep reportedly became "stoned" after eating the "cash crop"!

An earlier attempt to cultivate marijuana seeds on a rural property ended in failure, when he did not clear livestock from the paddock where the crop was growing. Sheep reportedly became "stoned" after eating the "cash crop"!

Peters hated Kyprie, whom he blamed for a $200,000 fraud scam that proved unsuccessful, and in April 1994 he was charged with conspiracy to murder Kyprie. He pleaded guilty to lesser charges which resulted in a five month sentence. This was later extended to nine months after he was found guilty of fraud. Peters was released from gaol before Thurgood-Dove was murdered, but claims that he knew nothing about the crime.

DEATH DIVE

Christine Watson was a bride of 11 days when she drowned off Townsville in October 2003. The 26-year-old American was participating in a diving excursion around the "Yongala" shipwreck with her new husband and experienced scuba diver, Gabe Watson. He later claimed that "We were together. Then I went up, and she went all the way down."

A dive expedition photographer claimed at the November 2007 inquest, that Gabe Watson returned to the tour boat shouting for help. Cardio Pulmonary Resuscitation (CPR) was then applied for 30 minutes, but the woman failed to respond.

...CPR was then applied for 30 minutes, but the woman failed to respond.

Suspicions about Gabe Watson's true role in his wife's death continued after he returned to Alabama, and in 2004 he was declared a murder suspect. His house was raided by local Federal Bureau of Investigation (FBI) agents and Queensland detectives. Documents, photographs and a computer that contained details about the diving trip were seized, and Watson was interviewed on at least 25 occasions.

He elected not to return to Australia for the subsequent Queensland inquest into Christine Watson's death. At the November 22nd hearing in 2007, approximately 65 witnesses provided personal or phone evidence in a complex case. However, in June 2009 Watson appeared before the Queensland Supreme Court in Brisbane pleading not guilty to murder but guilty to the lesser charge of manslaughter.

...the world's sporting media heralded the arrival of a new star.

Watson's plea was accepted and he spent 18 months behind bars with a suspended four-and-a-half year head sentence.

END OF A SPORTING LIFE

David Hookes made his international cricket debut in the 1977 Centenary Test between Australia and England, and the handsome, swashbuckling South Australian made a typically spectacular impact. The large MCG crowd roared its appreciation, when the 21-year-old left-hander blasted five successive boundaries from the bowling of English all-rounder Tony Greig, and the world's sporting media heralded the arrival of a new star.

By the time he retired as a player, Hookes had fallen a little short of the huge expectations that were initially placed on him. He averaged

David Hookes

a moderate 34.37 runs an innings as a batsman in his 23 Tests, and he struggled to maintain a regular position in the national team. He was considerably more successful at state level, where he became the highest run scorer in the Sheffield Shield competition.

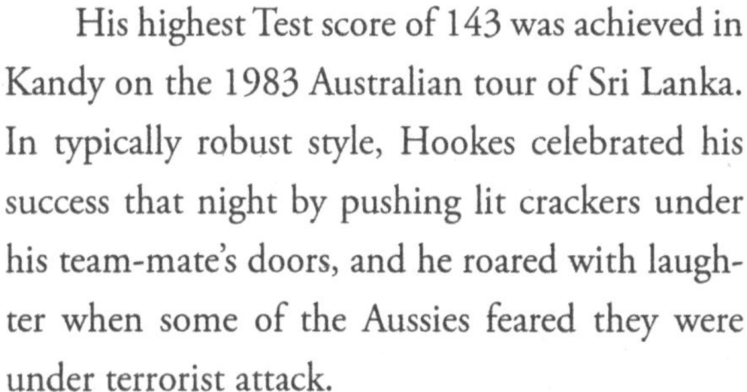

His highest Test score of 143 was achieved in Kandy on the 1983 Australian tour of Sri Lanka. In typically robust style, Hookes celebrated his success that night by pushing lit crackers under his team-mate's doors, and he roared with laughter when some of the Aussies feared they were under terrorist attack.

...she was called a "bitch" by a member of the security staff.

Strong leadership skills surfaced in his dynamic personality. He captained the previously last placed South Australia to a Sheffield Shield title in the 1981-82 seasons, and in 2003-04 he coached Victoria to victory in the same interstate competition. The twice married Hookes had become a renowned sports radio and TV commentator in Melbourne, when he met up with friends at St. Kilda's historic Beaconsfield Hotel, after coaching the Vics to victory against South Australia on 18th January 2004.

The party of 11 included players and officials from both teams, as well as four female partners. Copious amounts of alcohol were consumed by the boisterous group, until hotel bouncers started

Zdravko Micevic

calling "last drinks" around 11.30 pm. This move to end the evening began an altercation, which later produced a tragic outcome.

One female in the group was urged to "skol" her drink, and it was also alleged that she was called a "bitch" by a member of the security staff. The 50-year-old Hookes objected in typically provocative style, and allegedly threatened to criticise their actions on his radio program next day. He was placed in a headlock by bouncers, and escorted from the premises. Well known South Australian cricket identities in Darren Lehman and Wayne Phillips, both denied that they attempted to free their friend from the bouncers.

...collapsed heavily onto the road, and his head cracked like an egg.

Reports about what transpired after Hookes was ejected remain confusing. It is beyond dispute that after the rowdy cricket group vacated the hotel premises, a few bouncers continued to follow them for at least 70 metres up nearby Cowderoy Street. In the heated argument which developed, Victorian cricket identity Shaun Graf claimed that the bouncers were the aggressors, but this was disputed in court by Wayne Phillips.

There is no dispute about the tragic outcome from the feud. Twenty-one-year old bouncer Zdravko Micevic, a former Australian junior welterweight boxing champion, punched Hookes solidly with a left hook. The Victorian coach collapsed heavily onto the road, and his head cracked like an egg. Hookes never regained consciousness, and 24 hours later his family members agreed to remove hospital life support.

...Hookes hit him twice in the stomach before he retaliated.

Opinions differed again in the group about the exact circumstances of Hookes' death. Phillips did not see why his friend suddenly collapsed. Graf claimed that the Victorian coach said in protest "Hey, I'm out of your pub," before he was grabbed and then struck. Victorian player Rob Cassells supported Graf's view, and independent observers claimed that the attack by the bouncers was unexpected and unnecessary.

Public reaction to Hookes' death was strong and at times reached dangerous proportions. The home of the assailant was besieged with hate mail and personal threats to the Micevic family, who moved to another residence after receiving warnings that their house would be torched. Their house was set alight after being abandoned, and on 24th December 2004, the Beaconsfield Hotel closed its doors for the last time after operating for 124 years.

On 22nd August 2003, 19 months after the death of Hookes, Zdravko Micevic's manslaughter trial began in the Victorian Supreme Court. The defendant pleaded not guilty, claiming he was only defending himself when he struck Hookes. He also stated that Hookes hit

...after the bouncer stalked, and then fatally struck his victim...

him twice in the stomach before he retaliated. He denied that he lost his temper, and told the court that hotel management expected security staff to escort customers away from the premises, so that noise would be reduced.

Defence barrister Terry Forrest QC submitted that Hookes' "legendary status" was detrimental to the interests of his client, and submitted that the cricket group were unreliable and biased witnesses. He also successfully portrayed the evidence of a key witness as being prejudiced and self-serving. Micevic was well supported by the head of his security agency, who described the young bouncer as being "a role model of professionalism" in his usual dealings with the public.

Prosecution lawyers declared the fatal punch was delivered by an angry man, who pursued the provocative Hookes for nearly 100 metres from his accepted area of responsibility.

On 12th September 2005 the jury deliberated for seven hours before finding Zdravko not guilty of manslaughter. The decision surprised many who believed that a prosecution would result, after the bouncer stalked, and then fatally struck his victim, well away from his accepted area of responsibility.

Nothing can bring back the life of David Hookes, but six months after he was set free

Micevic was on hand to help the Australian boxing team in its preparation for the 2006 Commonwealth Games.

Did justice prevail?

Claire McDonald

WAS HIS DEATH JUSTIFIABLE?

...she was often forced to provide repugnant sexual acts for his gratification...

At first Claire Margaret McDonald claimed that she and her husband had a heated altercation with a stranger the night before he was found shot dead. However she soon changed her story, and admitted that it was she who shot Warren McDonald. The 38-year-old woman then provided police with graphic details, about years of continual physical and emotional abuse towards herself, and her five children, from a 40-year-old sadist.

Ms McDonald, a Victorian school teacher, revealed that she was often forced to provide repugnant sexual acts for his gratification, and that he frequently humiliated her children and herself in public. Her claims were strongly endorsed by a close friend, and even her in-laws supported these accusations to some extent. It took Claire McDonald 17 years of married hell to rectify the traumatic situation, but she was certainly focused in her intent when she finally took action.

On 30th November 2004, Claire McDonald phoned the house on the family's "Breakaway Mountain" property near Seymour, and told her son that she was stranded some distance away, because their land rover would not start. She left a message for his father about where to come to her aid, when he arrived home from work.

...methodically fired six times with her single shot rifle from about 50 metres...

She was dressed in Warren McDonald's camouflaged clothes, and hid for two hours while she waited for her prey to arrive. When her duped husband finally arrived and commenced tinkering with the vehicle, Claire McDonald methodically fired six times with her single shot rifle from about 50 metres, and fatally wounded her husband. While he bled to death Claire McDonald allegedly berated him for "making (me) do this".

At the trial which followed, the prosecution made much of the fact that Claire McDonald could have left the marriage or sought help from a women's refuge service. In 17 years of alleged abuse, she never took either option. He did not have to die for his behaviour, but that was the outcome that eventuated.

These telling observations fell on deaf ears, for on 3rd March 2006 Claire Margaret McDonald was cleared of both murder and manslaughter charges.

FAMILY COURT TRAUMAS

Custody battles between married and de facto couples are often intensely bitter and controversial. A 1998 survey revealed over 550,000 fathers believed that their custodial rights to their children were blatantly unfair. Non-custodial fathers tend to exhibit more desperate behaviour, with an average of at least one of this group committing suicide every day.

Violent murders sometimes erupts from these custodial battles, and from 1968-88, 48% of women slain in homicides were killed by their spouses or de facto partners. Sometimes the homicides include innocent, young children, with entire families being wiped out in revenge motivated slaughters.

...struck her on the back of the head with a sand-filled sock...

A DISTURBING CASE STUDY: PERTH FAMILY KILLINGS

In December 1978, Brian Altham, an Australian army major, waited near a Perth residence for his estranged wife Elizabeth to return home from a shopping expedition. When she returned, he struck her on the back of the head with a sand-filled sock, bound and gagged her, and bundled her into the back of his car.

Brian and Elizabeth Altham had then been separated for 12 months after a decade of marriage. Their two daughters, six-year-old Samantha and four-year-old Cherand were back in Brian's flat, where they usually spent their access visits. From there the two blonde headed children were collected, and the entire family was driven to a bush location.

...offered his wife a knife to slash her wrists.

There Elizabeth Altham was tied to a tree, and her husband drove away with their two daughters. Twenty minutes later he returned alone, and forcibly escorted his wife to a Vietnamese style bunker, which was supported by poles and a sheet of iron. Inside the structure was approximately three metres long, and a metre deep and wide.

Altham sealed the entrance with bricks, and offered his wife a knife to slash her wrists. After refusing the suicide option, Elizabeth was bound tightly and left to die from suffocation, while he attempted to overdose with copious amounts of sleeping tablets. Luckily she eventually wriggled herself free, and, after tying her sleeping husband's hands together, she removed the bricks from the bunker entrance and made her escape.

Eventually Elizabeth managed to flag

down a passing motorist from the nearby road, and she was taken to the nearby Brentwood police station. Before long a massive police search began, and after Brian Altham was found in a coma in the bunker, he was rushed to hospital. Similar bunkers were discovered nearby, with a fake bomb placed outside one as a decoy.

Meanwhile the search for the missing girls continued, and within two days everyone's worst fears were realised when their bodies were found in a bush grave about four kilometres from the bunker area. Both of them died after receiving severe head injuries with a hammer.

The Vietnam veteran attempted to hang himself in his prison cell before court proceedings began, but he survived his suicide bid. Brian Altham later pleaded not guilty on the grounds of insanity at his trial, but was found guilty of the double murders and sentenced to death. This decision was later commuted to life imprisonment.

...shot dead when she was flagging a taxi.

SUMMARY OF SIMILAR TRAGEDIES

A FAMILY COURT DECISION DIDN'T ADD UP

...killed his three children when they were with him on a holiday.

Margaret Case divorced Colin Case, a 52-year-old Darwin Mathematics teacher, but his ongoing harassment caused her to re-locate from the "Top End" to Adelaidc, where she became electorate secretary to Senator John Olsen. After Case threatened his 45-year-old former wife with an armed visit, the Family Court issued an injunction against him. A gaol term for this serious breech may have averted the tragic outcome which followed.

On 23rd March 1982, Margaret Case was shot dead when she was flagging a taxi. Two days later a badly dehydrated Case was arrested lying beside a dirt track.

In July 1993 Colin Case was sentenced to life imprisonment with a non-parole period of 20 years. If he had been placed in custody after breaching his injunction, there may have been a happier result.

IN THE WRONG PLACE

...in a frenzy of frustrated rage he stabbed her fatally four times.

On 8th July 1995, two policemen on the NSW North Coast, who had been assigned to protect Debra Minnett from the dangerous attention of 35-year-old John McGowan, were both shot dead. McGowan later killed himself.

SLAUGHTER IN THE NORTH

On 10th January 1996, Brisbane's Peter May killed his three children when they were with him on a holiday. Fifteen days later, after discovering the new abode of his estranged wife Helen, he killed her, both her parents, and finally himself.

RAGE KILLING IN DANDENONG

Fifty-four-year old Robert Parsons believed that his former de facto wife's maintenance demands were unjust, especially when she stipulated that he would be denied access to their children unless she received more financial help.

On the day their unresolved dispute went to court, Parsons claimed that she jeered at him in a nearby street, and in a frenzy of frustrated rage he stabbed her fatally four times. For this crime he received a sentence of life imprisonment on 24th May, 1999.

DIFFICULT TO BE FAIR

In 1997 a woman sought to move herself and her children from Cairns to Bendigo, where she intended to re-marry and settle. This proposal was opposed in court by her ex-husband, on the grounds that such a move would effectively deny him access to his children.

The Full Bench of the Family Court decided in the wife's favour.

...killed by a bomb explosion after she opened a door of her house.

DANGERS ASSOCIATED WITH FAMILY COURT DECISIONS

In 1969 De Silvano Marite married a woman 19 years younger than himself. The relationship became strained, and after she was admitted to Hornsby Hospital in 1978 with injuries attributed to her husband, she was awarded custody of their three children.

A devastated Marite attempted to stow away with the children to Singapore during an access visit, but was detained and gaoled for 12 months for contempt of court.

Justice David Opas, who originally awarded custody of the children to the wife, was subsequently shot dead on 23rd June 1980, after he answered the door bell at his Sydney family home.

...sued the newspaper after it was revealed that her name was included in "Evil Scum".

In July of that year Marite was refused all access to his children by Justice Richard Gee in the Family Court. On 6th March 1984, Gee received lacerations to his legs, arms and face after his house was rocked by a huge explosion.

A little over a month later a bomb explosion caused extensive damage to the Family Court Registry in Parramatta. Marite was interviewed by police after he was found nearby issuing a pamphlet titled "Evil Scum", which strongly criticised several Family Court judges.

Then, in July 1984, 55-year-old Pearl Watson, the wife of Justice Ray Watson, was killed by a bomb explosion after she opened a door of her house. Justice Watson was knocked unconscious in the same incident. Marite again successfully denied his guilt, and on 2nd May 1987 an open finding was delivered on the death of Pearl Watson.

The pamphlet situation then resurfaced, when Justice Evatt successfully sued the "Sun Herald" newspaper for deformation, after it was revealed that her name was included in "Evil

Scum". Marite did not provide evidence.

In August 1984, Marite was summoned to appear before the Federal Court before Justice Elliott. Marite refused to apologise to his wife for publicly insulting her, and received a suspended sentence of three months. In more recent times Marite, along with other Family Court detractors, was questioned about the bombing death of Graham Wise, a 37-year-old father of three.

CHAPTER SEVEN:

CORRUPTION, INCOMPETENCE & FEUDS

The infamous Rum Rebellion of colonial times featured an illegal alignment of law enforcement figures, criminals and the controlling political elite. While this period was a black spot in the integrity of Australian history, some experts believe that the misuse of power observed in NSW between 1965–1976 was even more corrupt in its magnitude.

The Liberal-Country Coalition parties governed the state then, and the corruption of politicians and elements of the police force was widespread. Fred Hansen was Police Commissioner for some of those years, and it is rumoured that he received $100,000 a year in bribes from just one illegal casino.

It is also claimed then that "R.A.", (NSW Premier Sir Robert Askin), received bribes of up to $30,000 a month from the 33 Club. Noted academic Dr Alfred McCoy was especially trenchant in his criticism of the scope of corruption.

Juanita Nielsen

"No city in the world could rival Sydney's tolerance for organised crime ...from 1965-76... the state endured a period of political corruption unparalleled in its modern history".

In later year Queensland became similarly tainted, and after the Fitzgerald Commission revealed the extent of illegal practices that had developed in the Sunshine State", Police Commissioner Sir Terrence Lewis was stripped of his honours and titles and gaoled for corruption.

A PERMANENT SOLUTION

"No city in the world could rival Sydney's toler-ance for organised crime..."

On 4th July 1975 Juanita Nielsen, a wealthy heiress, Sydney newspaper publisher and anti-development campaigner, was last seen in the Kings Cross area where she had arranged a business appointment. On that day Juanita Nielsen vanished, and 30 years later her disappearance remains one of Australia's greatest unsolved mysteries.

Was it anti-development activities that led to her demise, or the alleged dossiers she had on prominent peoples' links to corruption, criminal involvement and sexual deviation? Any one of these scenarios is possible, and key figures linked to this vexed case include:

LORETTA CRAWFORD

Frank Theeman

A drag queen and nightclub receptionist and the last reported person to see Juanita Nielsen alive. When questioned further about what she observed, Crawford referred to an unknown third man who was present with Juanita and Eddie Trigg, the man Nielsen agreed to meet that day.

FRANK THEEMAN

A once powerful figure who in 1970 reportedly sold his women's clothing business for a hefty $3.5 million and became heavily involved in property development. Theeman founded the Victoria Point Company which aimed to re-develop the area of Sydney between Potts Point and Kings Cross. This multi-million dollar project threatened the homes and lifestyle of many poor people in Sydney's Victoria Street, and Juanita Nielsen became a fierce opponent of Theeman's development plans.

...multi-million dollar project threatened the homes and lifestyle of many poor people...

She received such strong support from the powerful Builders' Labourers Union that Theeman's plans were stalled, and his considerable wealth evaporated after he reportedly lost millions on the failed development project.

The Victoria Street Action group later linked Theeman to Juanita Nielsen's disappearance. Detective-Sergeant Karl Arkins questioned him

Abe Saffron

about the missing heiress, but soon after that interview took place Arkins was removed from the case, presumably at the behest of Police Commissioner Hanson.

JAMES ANDERSON

Jim Anderson was once described by one of his many detractors as being "a blot on the name of Sydney". The Scottish born Anderson soon became a powerful and controversial figure after arriving in Sydney in 1959. He became the manager of the Venus Club, a Kings Cross establishment he leased from criminal heavyweight Abe Saffron, with whom he came to share a mutual hatred. Saffron became a close crony of Deputy Police Commissioner Bill Allen, but in later years the National Crime Authority (NCA) provided a generous retainer for Anderson to help uncover damning evidence against Saffron.

..."self defence", even though one of the gunshot wounds was found in the back of the deceased.

On 22nd June 1970, Anderson shot dead another criminal. The killing was deemed to be "self defence", even though one of the gunshot wounds was found in the back of the deceased. The death occurred in the Latin Quarter of Kings Cross in the presence of police. No charges were laid – Anderson's influential role as a regular police informer appeared to provide him with immunity from prosecution.

EDDIE TRIGG & SHAYNE MARTIN-SIMMONDS

Eddie Trigg

Eddie Trigg supposedly set up a July 4th meeting in 1975 with Juanita Nielsen to discuss advertising arrangements in "NOW", a publication that Nielsen edited. Shayne Martin-Simmonds and his girlfriend Marilyn King (who started life as Arthur King), were also alleged to have been present.

Three days after Nielsen disappeared, a road maintenance gang found Juanita's black leather handbag on the side of a road. A few days later a tube of lipstick, a felt pen and other items from her handbag were found scattered further along the road side. No finger print matches were revealed from police files.

...a road maintenance gang found Juanita's black leather handbag on the side of a

Real estate agent Glenn Williams later claimed that he saw Juanita Nielsen join two men in a yellow coloured Ford. A car of this type was unknown to Ms Nielsen's friends, and police later discounted this lead, even though Williams' recollection of one of the men closely resembled a description of Shayne Martin-Simmonds.

Marilyn King

In September 1975, Marilyn King revealed that Twigg and Martin-Simmonds earlier attempted to lure Ms Nielsen to the Camperdown Travel Lodge. Eddie Twigg disappeared when investigations intensified, but Martin-Simmonds was charged and later found guilty of conspiring

...$70,000 would be paid into his account for pleading guilty...

to abduct Juanita Nielsen. He was subsequently released after serving one year in custody.

Twigg was arrested in San Francisco in mid 1982, and on 1st February 1983 he pleaded guilty to the conspiracy charge, much to the surprise of his legal representative, Stuart Littlemore. At the time Twigg denied any knowledge of the rumour that $70,000 would be paid into his account for pleading guilty to the conspiracy charge, which also resulted in "no names" of other suspects being divulged. Twigg was sentenced to three years in custody with a minimum non-parole period of 15 months.

In August 1983 an inquest was conducted into the case. It was found that there was no evidence to support a prima face case for an indictable offence against any person. The possibility, however, of police corruption being a factor in the Nielsen case, was not discounted.

In recent times some public figures, including media personality Wendy Harmer, have received threats after making fresh allegations about the Juanita Nielsen case which still remains unsolved.

OVERSEAS IMPORTS

Criminal elements have been involved with many immigrant communities in Australia since the first group of foreigners arrived in 1788. Since then various ethnic groups of villains have tended to specialise in areas of crime.

The Italian "Mafia", have been heavily involved in the cultivation and trafficking of marijuana. Money laundering and protection rackets have also been focuses of interest.

Powerful Chinese triads have controlled as much as 85% of the national heroin market, while Lebanese gangs have also been active in that field. Korean criminals have favoured prostitution and loan sharking, and many Vietnamese criminals traffic heroin.

...200 witnesses claimed they saw nothing when Duang Van Chu was gunned down...

Violent gangland feuds have often erupted among various groups. Stanley Wong, who was then called the "unofficial mayor of Chinatown" in Sydney, was robbed and killed by two illegal Asian immigrants in 1985. In 1992 approximately 200 witnesses claimed they saw nothing when Duang Van Chu was gunned down, and in December of the same year a 16-year-old student was beaten to death in a reprisal attack by the 5T gang.

Fear of reprisals, especially in Asian communities, have often thwarted police probes into organised crime. Bookmaker Lloyd Tidmarsh was slain in his own home, and within the space of three years there were 265 domestic invasions reported in Sydney alone.

A code of silence frustrated police after approximately $20,000,000 was stolen from the Haymarket branch of the NBA in the Christmas holiday period of 1987. Most of the customers were from the local Chinese community, and the fear of reprisals, as well as the possibility of tax office investigations, resulted in little useful information being divulged

Vietnamese immigrants began settling around Cabramatta and other areas of Sydney shortly after Communist forces took control of their native country. Many young Vietnamese students applied themselves diligently to their studies, and names such as Nguyen and Minh featured prominently in matriculation and university results.

...carried a firearm from the age of 11 and was involved in a murder when he was 14...

Other youths, such as 18-year-old Minh Hong, chose the path of crime, and many people in his community were bashed and robbed. Violence increased, and in a gangland feud Minh Hoang Nguyen and Dinh Ngo were killed in a restaurant shoot-out. In October 1988 prominent gangland leader Nghai Minh Hong was also fatally wounded after falling out with a rival gang.

Tri Minh Tran, who carried a firearm from the

age of 11 and was involved in a murder when he was 14, became one of the most ruthless gang leaders in the Vietnamese community. He was killed in his own flat by a rival faction of the 5T gang.

A decade before, after several people were wounded in a Sydney club, all of the 279 patrons declared they knew nothing about the attacks, because they were all in one of the four toilets on the premises!

AUSTRALIA'S FIRST POLITICAL ASSASSINATION

...deportation of the most violent criminals in Vietnamese and Chinese communities...

Around that time State ALP Member John Newman became a public champion for Vietnamese migrants. His support for respectable hard working elements around Cabramatta attracted adverse attention from the 5T gang, whose involvements in heroin distribution, protection rackets and home invasions were threatened.

Newman's car was paint bombed and threats were issued as his anti-crime crusade intensified. Newman called for the deportation of the most violent criminals in Vietnamese and Chinese communities, regardless of their citizenship status, and on 5th September 1994 the criminal community struck back.

Newman had arrived home that night from

a local ALP branch meeting, and he and his fiancée Lucy Wang were placing a protective cover over his car in the driveway when he was shot twice in his chest.

Australians were shocked by the nation's first political assassination, and at first Tri Ninh Tran was the main suspect. He was widely suspected of previously issuing death threats to the Member for Cabramatta, but eventually it was Phuong Ngo, the owner of the Mekong nightclub, who was arrested and charged with Newman's murder.

Ngo's club was rumoured to be a gambling den and money laundering centre...

Phuong Ngo then became the focus of a long legal process. One former trial was aborted, while another resulted in a hung jury, but finally on 29th June 2001 the former Fairfield councillor was found guilty of the murder of John Newman. Ngo's club was rumoured to be a gambling den and money laundering centre. He allegedly felt threatened by Newman's anti-crime campaign.

The gunman has never been found but Phuong Ngo is now imprisoned in the maximum security section of Goulburn

The conviction of Phuong Ngo, together with the murder of Tri Ninh Tran, weakened the 5T gang which gradually lost its previous influence in local crime activities.

SOMETHING ROTTEN IN AUSTRALIA'S NORTH

...found Lewis guilty of accepting bribes totalling $700,000 as protection money...

By the 1980s accusations about political police corruption in Queensland were rife, and it was Terrence Murray Lewis who became the centre of much controversy.

Lewis was born in February 1928, and after joining the state police force he rose quickly through the ranks and finally became the Queensland Police Commissioner. He held this prestigious position for 12 years between 1975–1987, and received a knighthood during his term of office.

Many concerned observers, however, noted his close links with disgraced former Commissioner Francis Bischof, and in 1987, when Assistant Commissioner Graeme Parker confessed that Lewis and he were also involved in corrupt practices, the enviable lifestyle of the police knight began to unravel.

The Fitzgerald Commission was established and after its investigation was completed in 1989. Sir Terence Lewis was charged with 23 counts of perjury, corruption and forgery. After five months of hearing evidence, and five days of consideration by the appointed jury, a District Court found Lewis guilty of accepting bribes totalling $700,000 as protection money from brothels,

SP bookies, illegal casinos and line operators opposing the legalisation of poker machines in Queensland.

He was also found guilty of forging the signature of the State Premier Sir Joh Bjelke-Petersen on an official police document in 1981. Judge Tony Healy sentenced him to 14 years gaol with a minimum period of nine years and six months.

Lewis was also found not guilty of lying to the Commission, and he was acquitted on seven perjury charges.

On 26th March 1993 Terry Lewis became only the 14th person in Australia's history to be stripped of his knighthood, and all other honours previously bestowed were also removed.

Lewis was released from custody in 2002 after many unsuccessful appeals against his convictions.

It took six appeals over many years before Darryl Beamish was cleared on a charge of a murder...

WOES OF THE WEST

Perth, bordered by the Indian Ocean on its western terrain, and the vast, arid Nullabor Plain to the east, is arguably the most isolated city in the world.

State-wide the huge area of 2.5 million kilometres, results in Western Australia (WA) being the largest area of police responsibility in the world – a highly relevant fact when the competence of the WA force is being debated. However there is still cause for concern about incidents of bungling, cronyism and stubbornness that has prevailed both in WA policing and judicial decisions now for some time.

Jillian Brewer

It took six appeals over many years before Darryl Beamish was cleared on a charge of a murder that was later attributed to notorious serial killer, Eric Cooke. The then 19-year-old Beamish is a deaf mute, but the Macro Task Force that conducted investigations questioned him without a trained interpreter being present.

She was fatally run down by a car after arguing with her then boyfriend...

Beamish's alibi was discounted, he was found guilty of murdering chocolate manufacturer heiress, Jillian Brewster, and he was sentenced to death. The young man spent a traumatic four months on death row, before his sentence was commuted to life imprisonment. Beamish served 15 years in custody, despite the fact that Cooke confessed to the murder before being hung in October, 1964.

Cooke is crucially linked to another WA miscarriage of justice. In February 1963, John Button was convicted of killing his girlfriend Rosemary Anderson. She was fatally run down by a car after arguing with her then 19-year-old boyfriend, for which Button served a ten year sentence. A reprieve for the accused man appeared likely after Cooke confessed to the hit and run murder before facing the gallows, but police dis-

Darryl Beamish

missed the serial killer's testimony.

Button was released five years after his sentence had been reduced to manslaughter. He married soon after gaining freedom, but the traumas associated with his unjust imprisonment weighed heavily on him. Button tried to commit suicide in 1977, and after this failed attempt he became deeply religious.

He unsuccessfully took his case to the WA Appeals Board where journalist Estelle Blackburn took a special interest in his welfare after hearing the evidence presented. Blackburn began tracking down victims who had been injured during Cooke's hit and run rampage, and she used this research to write a book titled "Broken Lives".

...from the age of 13 she had been sexually abused for four years by an ex-football star.

Blackburn's new revelations forced the WA Appeals Court tore-open Button's case in 1999, and in March that year he was cleared of all charges. Cooke was named as the likely killer of Rosemary Anderson, and the 57-year-old Button announced his intention to become an Elder in the Presbyterian Church.

Rumours about police and political corruption surfaced after Perth brothel madam, Shirley Finn (dubbed "the Queen of vice") was murdered by a person or persons unknown in 1975, and twenty years later the controversial Andrew Mallard case occurred. Mallard was convicted for the murder of a Perth jeweller in 1995, and a decade later this case was also quashed by the state Director of Public Prosecutions (DPP).

In 1998 a young woman informed police that from the age of 13 she had been sexually abused for four years by an ex-football star. On 10th November of that year Superintendent Dave Caporn allegedly instructed the officer in charge of the case to release the man until the evidence was properly examined. The accused was not charged, and the alleged victim was never interviewed.

...fell to his death on a freeway from a pedestrian footbridge.

Confused judicial decisions continued with the Phillip Walsham case. On 27th February 1998, the heavily intoxicated 21-year-old Walsham fell to his death on a freeway from a pedestrian footbridge. Earlier that evening, Salvotore Fazzari, Jose Martinez and Carlos Pereiras had attacked Walsham, outside a suburban train station

The trio were first charged with assault, but two years later that charge was upgraded to murder, and in March 2004 they were convicted of either throwing or pushing Walsham to his death.

All three defendants pleaded guilty to assaulting Walsham earlier on the evening he died, but innocent to the charge of murder. They admitted to kicking and punching Walsham around the head during an argument, but claimed that the assaulted man was alive when they departed from the scene. Their defence lawyers submitted that, following the assault, Walsham accidentally fell from the bridge to the road below, and that his life ended when he was struck by a hit and run driver.

Despite the speculative and circumstantial quality of the prosecution's evidence, the trio were found guilty, and sentenced to ten years in gaol. Subsequently strong public lobbying against the decision, instigated mainly by the girlfriend of one of the accused, has resulted in the verdict being quashed by the Court of Appeal in July 2007.

"The DPP is the worst in Australia by the length of the Nullabor Strait."

In November 2001, Canadian Rory Christian's Australian wife Susan disappeared. Christian was later found guilty of her murder, despite the fact that no body was found. Two tears later he was released from gaol after the case was dismissed at a re-trial.

Such examples indicate why the competence of the WA law enforcement system is still debated fiercely in the public domain. A 2001 opinion poll showed that Western Australia was 6% below the national average confidence rates in law enforcement procedures.

State Labor MP John Quigley believes that this finding accurately reflects community disenchantment in the West.

"The DPP is the worst in Australia by the length of the Nullabor Strait." He stated bluntly after the Walsham case was aborted.

Other spokesman, however, sprang to the defence of the DPP.

"It is not about winning or losing," stated Chris Dawson, the WA Deputy Police Commissioner, after the Walsham case was quashed. "(it is) about justice being determined in the proper way."

The then Acting Director of the DPP, Ken Bates, was also quick to defend his organisation.

"(It is) unfair to judge the system on the basis of a couple of high profile cases over 40 years alone, when one considers the huge volume of cases (that come to trial)."

In the West, "the jury is still out on a verdict" about the competence of law enforcement agencies.

In the West, "the jury is still out on a verdict" about the competence of law enforcement agencies.

POLICE FEUD IN VICTORIA

On February 8th 2008, retired Federal Court Judge Murray Wilcox QC, delivered a commissioned report to the Victorian Parliament. Following his intense investigation into police corruption, Wilcox recommended that the Office of Public Prosecution (OPP) consider charging three senior police officers.

The officers he named were the Police Association Secretary Paul Mullett, former Assistant

Commissioner Noel Ashby, and former Police Media Director Stephen Linnell. Mullett stated on 15th February 2008, after previously being suspended by Police Commissioner Christine Nixon, that he would not seek a renewal of his position when his current contract expired in March 2009. The other accused officers resigned from their positions shortly after accusations against the trio were revealed in late 2007.

Ashby and Linnell were accused of perjury, lying to the Office of Police Integrity (OPI), and misconduct in public office. Mullett was to answer charges on these issues, as well as an accusation that he attempted to pervert the course of justice, however none of the charges were to stick, and he retired from the police force in 2009. Other officers who were also under scrutiny include Inspector Glenn Weir and Police Association President Brian Rix.

...he was able to negotiate directly about important police issues with then Premier, Steve Bracks...

Wilcox described Mullett as the "puppet master", who sought to have Ashby become his "puppet commissioner" when Nixon and her Assistant Police Commissioner, Simon Overland, were undermined so badly by an orchestrated campaign, that they would be forced to resign. Linnell was described as a crony of the pair, who passed on confidential information that would increase Mullett's power and aid the negative campaign.

Paul Mullett, a man who formerly won two bravery awards as a serving policeman, became so influential in police politics that he was able to negotiate directly about important police issues with then Premier, Steve Bracks, prior to the last state elections. He still enjoyed the support of the Police Association after he was discredited, but his position became virtually untenable after Nixon and subsequent Premier John Brumby, refused to negotiate with him.

It was alleged that Ashby, when he was Assistant Commissioner, leaked confidential information in a taped phone call to Mullett, about Detective Peter Lalor, (a close friend of Mullett's) being a suspect in the Shane Chartres-Abbott murder case.

...a male prostitute, who may have implicated Lalor, was shot dead before his evidence was submitted in court.

In 2007 Chartres-Abbott, a male prostitute, was about to face trial for rape, and investigating police believe that his killing was an act of revenge.

In early 2008 the Melbourne Age revealed that the confidential tax records and address of the murdered male prostitute, were unlawfully accessed from confidential files before the gangland hitman gunned Chartres-Abbott down.

Subsequently a police task force code named Briars, began investigating the contract killer's claims that Detective Lalor accessed the address of the male prostitute. He also provided a quazi alibi for the assailant on the day of the murder.

The hitman, who is already serving a life sentence until 2023 will allegedly serve no extra time in prison after implicating corrupt policeman in the execution plan.

By April 2008 further action in the murder probe was stymied after Lalor refused to attend an internal discipline hearing. Since being suspended on full pay in September 2007, he has found other employment in the building industry.

CHAPTER EIGHT:

TWO "LADIES IN A ROGUES" GALLERY

DULCIE MARKHAM

Also known as "the blonde bombshell" that lost eight lovers and two husbands to killers' bullets in the late 1940s and early 1950s.

Markham inspired a machine gun battle near the MCG in the 1950s, and she reportedly called fondly "Good-bye sweetheart", when a new admirer was led to his gaol cell after killing one of her other lovers.

Dulcie Markham, who allegedly became a respectable housewife, perished in a 1976 house fire after she fell asleep while smoking.

PETTINGILL CLAN

In her heyday Kath Pettingill was known as "Granny Evil". The former brothel madam spawned and raised the cream of Melbourne's armed robbers, drug dealers, police informers and murderers among her offspring, before retiring to

Dennis Allen

the peaceful coastal hamlet of Venus Bay where the following sign allegedly welcomed visitors to her home.

"Premises protected by shotgun three days a week. Guess which three!"

DENNIS ALLEN

The most vicious of Kath Pettingill's notorious sons, who was definitely connected with two murders and believed to have been involved in as many as 12. He reportedly used a chainsaw to dismember up Hells Angel biker Anton Kenny, and Allen was also responsible for over 30 armed robberies.

The information that he provided to police kept him free from custody, but Allen died prematurely from a heart condition when his name was still feared in underworld circles.

"Premises protected by shotgun three days a week. Guess which three!"

VICTOR GEORGE PEIRCE

Another one of Kath Pettingill's dubious sons, who was one of a group controversially found not guilty after two young constables were executed in South Yarra. The double murder was allegedly a revenge killing following the police shooting of armed robber Graeme Jensen, a friend of the group.

Drug dealing and armed robbery were Peirce's usual criminal pursuits, but the cocky braggart became careless once he started taking ecstasy pills to relieve the boredom of working on Melbourne's wharves. Peirce was reportedly in debt to the tune of $30,000 when he was shot dead in his car in May 2002 at Port Melbourne. He had also reneged on a contract agreement to murder Jason Moran.

Carl Williams was believed to have ordered the execution of Peirce, and the gunman hired to carry out the killing was Andrew "Benji" Veniamin.

GRAHAM "THE MUNSTER" KINNIBURGH

An old style criminal who mostly lived a quiet life in the affluent Melbourne suburb of Kew. In his youth Kinniburgh was a safe breaker par excellence who led the Magnetic Drill gang which stole millions of dollars in various successful heists.

...led the Magnetic Drill gang which stole millions of dollars in various successful heists.

"The Munsters' neighbours regarded him as a quiet law abiding citizen, so it came as no surprise when Kinniburgh's well educated son chose the prestigious and venue of Melbourne's Windsor Hotel for his wedding reception.

Guests from the top end of town were puzzled when menacing looking men wearing dark sunglasses mingled with the other guests. A property developer, who was deemed to be paying too much attention to one of the gang baron's female guests, suddenly lost all interest in dancing after he was advised to either become a wallflower or end up being shot. Kinniburgh's daughter also enjoyed a "high society" wedding when she married the son of a Melbourne QC and prominent state politician.

"had enough enemies to fill a telephone book"

Graham Kinniburgh's life ended when he was gunned down in his driveway after he returned home from walking his dog. Carl Williams was the rival who organised his murder, and once again "Benji" Veniamin was the trigger man.

MARK MORAN

Mark Moran

Before his death Mark Moran feared that he was a marked man in the Melbourne gangland war that was being waged by Carl Williams. On two occasions before he was gunned down, Mark Moran was hospitalised with bouts of depression. He confided then to a male friend that the violent excesses of his younger half- brother Jason were endangering the welfare of the Moran family.

JASON MORAN

Jason Moran

An unpredictable and violent criminal who "had enough enemies to fill a telephone book". His biggest mistake was to inflict only a stomach wound on Carl Williams instead of shooting his future rival in the head, which is what Mark Moran recommended. If Williams had been executed, a Melbourne gangland war that cost at least 29 lives over an eight-year period, might have been averted.

Jason Moran and his unlucky friend Pasquale Barbaro were both shot dead by a masked gunman while they watched a junior football clinic at Essendon. Five children were also in the car, but they were physically unharmed during the dual gangland murders.

...both shot dead by a masked gunman while they watched a junior football clinic...

LEWIS MORAN

Lewis Moran

The father of Mark and Jason Moran who for decades was heavily involved in Melbourne's drug trade. Lewis Moran was gunned down in a Brunswick club.

CARL WILLIAMS

Graham Kinniburgh, Mario Condello, Mick Gatto and other established barons of Melbourne crime treated Williams as a bumptious upstart. This attitude gravely underestimated the growing influence of the ambitious young criminal who dubbed himself "the premier".

Carl Williams

The spate of killings in the battle for power between Williams' group and the "Carlton Crew" escalated into dangerous proportions, even by Melbourne's underworld standards. The old guard of criminals were shocked when Williams permanently removed Kinniburgh, Lewis Moran, Willie Thompson and Michael Marshall in quick succession.

...confessed to the gangland murders of an anonymous drug dealer...

However the probability of living behind the repressive walls of Barwon Prison's maximum security section for the rest of his life broke down "The Premier's" resistance. The killer who once boasted that "I run this f...... state", confessed to the gangland murders of an anonymous drug dealer, as well as Jason and Lewis Moran, in the hope that he would avoid facing trial for as many as ten murders.

Judge Betty King was unimpressed by Williams' bid for lenient treatment, and in May 2007 she sentenced him to life imprisonment with a non-parole period of 35 years.

She denied "The Premier" a right of reply and his "term in office" abruptly ended. However, in 2010 Williams was beaten to death by fellow inmate Matthew Charles Johnson, who used the stem of an exercise bike to batter his victim.

TONY MOKBEL

Tony Mokbel

Antonius Jajih Mokbel first established links with Carl Williams, "the Raptor" and "Goggles" at Port Phillip Prison. Subsequently Mokbel's heavy involvement in Melbourne's burgeoning drug trade proved to be extremely lucrative. However when he was unexpectedly granted bail on a cocaine trafficking charge, Mokbel was also warned that more serious charges were pending.

Tony Mokbel learned that he was to be co-charged with Carl Williams for the Lewis Moran and Michael Marshall murders, and the son of a Lebanese migrant then began "a life on the run".

Tony Mokbel needed to be lucky every day he was on the run; his Pirana Task Force pursu-ers only needed to be lucky on one day.

For nearly 15 months he evaded police capture, first in a remote Victorian country property and later in Greece where he fled on a false passport. In Athens Mokbel linked up with his Australian de facto wife and family, and he continued to manage his drug trafficking interests from his overseas base. However, soon after Mokbel allegedly purchased a Greek shipping company, his months of freedom ended.

Since April 2007 a staggering $1,000,000 reward was on offer for information leading to the drug baron's arrest, and Victorian police were confident that this enticing lure would ultimately result in the arrest of the cocky fugitive. Tony Mokbel needed to be lucky every day he was on the run; his Purana Task Force pursuers only needed to be lucky on one day.

The elusive criminal's luck ran out when Greek police, acting on a tip-off from Australia, arrested Mokbel at a trendy Athens café. By then Mokbel had grown a beard, and he also wore an unconvincing wig. By late February 2008, it was alleged that Mokbel was informally negotiating with Victorian police from his Athens gaol in the hope of gaining as little as a 25-year-sentence for drug trafficking.

Despite his attempts to avoid extradition, Mokbel faced court in Victoria in 2012, and received a 30 year sentence for his crimes. In 2019, he was stabbed by fellow inmates at Barwon prison — an attack he barely survived.

"THE RAPTOR" AND "GOGGLES"

Two notorious "hit men" and armed robbers who allegedly accepted a down payment of two kilograms of speed, a pair of handguns and $20,000 for one of the killings ordered by Williams and Mokbel.

Pirana Task Force officers installed listening devices in the gunmen's getaway car, which led to their arrest shortly after the Marshall murder. Former Melbourne detective Brian "Skull" Murphy considers that the infamous pair was safer in their Barwon Prison cells following their arrest for this murder. "Better to be tried by 12 than carried out by six", was his succinct assessment of their vulnerability in the gangland war.

...accepted a down payment of two kilograms of speed, a pair of handguns and $20,000 for one of the killings...

However by the autumn of 2006, after enduring almost two years of mind numbing lockdown conditions in the Acacia Unit, both men admitted their guilt. "The Raptor", who had previously executed at least three victims, provided evidence that implicated both Williams and Mokbel in murder and conspiracy to murder charges.

Further damaging evidence was readily provided by "The Gunsmith", a third accomplice who was facing the possibility of 23 years in lock-down conditions for committing three murders when he had not actually fired a shot. He had provided two sawn off shotguns to Williams, but was not directly involved in the executions. Carl Williams also admitted to three murders in the hope that he would not live out the rest of his life in the solitary confinement type conditions of the Acacia Unit.

"Better to be tried by 12 than carried out by six"

TERRY HODSON

A narcotics dealer who allegedly became involved in illegal business dealings with David Michel, a Detective-Sergeant with the drug squad. In September 2004 it is believed that the pair tried to burgle a house that supposedly contained 1.3 million dollars worth of drugs which police intended to seize.

The would-be burglars were foiled by a neighbour's call to police, and Michel was savaged by a police dog when he attempted to escape. Hodson surrendered at the crime scene and offered to provide evidence against Michel and Tony Mokbel.

The drug squad had access to narcotics that could earn them the equivalent of an annual salary in just one weekend, and Paul Dale, another drug squad detective involved with Williams and Mokbel, was also suspected of being involved in the Hodson case. Dale has since left the police force and is now rumoured to be managing a petrol service station in Victoria's north-east

The drug squad had access to narcotics that could earn them the equivalent of an annual salary in just one weekend...

During Hodson's police interview process Michel, who had been involved in a relationship with the drug dealer's daughter, allegedly forwarded Hodson a card which contained a picture of an executed American gangster.

As the questioning of Hodson became more intense, anxiety rose among corrupt policemen and the Williams-Mokbel group, and on 16th May 2004 the executed bodies of Terry Hodson and his wife Christine were found in their East Kew home. Police investigators believe that the killers were known to the Hodson family as there were no signs of forced entry into the premises.

This atrocity caused state opposition members and the Victorian Bar Association to call for a judicial enquiry into police corruption.

The government responded by granting the state ombudsman sweeping powers similar to a Royal Commission in status, and the Purana Task Force recently began to check the financial earnings of reputed criminals.

Mario Condello

MARIO CONDELLO

A corrupt lawyer who took over the reigns of power in the "Carlton Crew" when Mick Gatto was in remand for the shooting of Andrew Veniaman. During the height of Melbourne's underworld war Condello and George Defteros were charged with conspiracy to murder Carl Williams, his drug dealing father George, and an unnamed third party. Condello had the reputation of being one of the most effective money launderers in the state, and this exceedingly vain man also had a deep respect for Italian underworld traditions.

The alarm bells should have sounded for Condello after two contract killers were arrested near his heavily fortressed suburban home. However he ignored such ominous incidents and continued to live the same lifestyle, before he was shot dead in his own garage on 6th February 2006.

...two contract killers were arrested near his heavily fortressed suburban home...

Mark "Chopper" Read

"CHOPPER" QUIPS

Mark "Chopper" Read who was once the most feared enforcer in Pentridge Gaol's maximum security division, rivalled Ned Kelly as a celebrity.

He formerly survived a murderous attack in custody from the much feared Gregory "Bluey" Brazel, as well as many other attempts on his life.

Mark Read wrote many best sellers, including children's books, and crime writers John Silvester and Andrew Rule remain famous for the revelations they produced in their book titled "Chopper From The Inside". "Chopper" himself described his own writings as "faction" – a mixture of a few facts merged with fiction.

The black humour of this larger than life figure, who cut off his own ears to briefly exchange a hospital bed for a gaol cell, was enjoyed by many who have heard "Chopper" Read at his numerous public speaking engagements. He once confided to a receptive audience that "I love to spread a picnic rug out on the banks of the Yarra and watch all my enemies float by."

...cut off his own ears to briefly exchange a hospital bed for a gaol cell...

"Chopper" was also involved in business promotions, and the following slogan has been used to market a beer brand that he personally endorsed.

"Chopper Heavy" – a beer 100% guaranteed to get your ears off.

Chopper Read died from liver cancer, aged 58, in October 2013.

"I love to spread a picnic rug out on the banks of the Yarra and watch all my enemies float by."

CHAPTER NINE:

FAMILY TIES

SEEING DOUBLE

Police in Victoria were mystified. How could banks or TABs, hundreds of kilometres apart, be robbed simultaneously at gunpoint by robbers answering the same description? For years during the 1970s this question remained unanswered, until Peter Morgan was arrested after shooting and nearly killing a policeman during a 1979 bank robbery at suburban Edithvale.

Investigators learned that Morgan had an identical twin, and after Douglas Morgan was apprehended on a property in rural West Gippsland their armed robbery tactics were revealed.

The Morgan twins coordinated their robberies simultaneously to confuse police and lessen the chances of detection. Both served custodial sentences after being charged. Peter and Douglas Morgan are now believed to be employed in the building trade.

A BROTHER TO DIE FOR

Paul Heatley took on significant risks when he agreed to assist his brother in a 1994 warehouse robbery. Unfortunately the gamble "misfired" with fatal consequences.

..."road rage" shooting which occurred because Dunn threw a bottle at Heatley's car.

Earl Heatley was a hardened and violent criminal. In 1981 he was released after serving a long custodial sentence for the murder of Robert Francis Dunn. It was a "road rage" shooting which occurred because Dunn threw a bottle at Heatley's car.

The released man then became involved in the trading of illicit drugs, and Earl Heatley targeted that particular warehouse in 1994 as he believed the premises contained chemicals he needed to manufacture amphetamines.

In actuality no money or valuables were on hand, and tragically two lives were lost in the botched robbery. After a masked and armed Earl Heatley burst into the premises his brother Paul wrestled the factory owner to the floor. Indiscriminate shooting from Earl Heatley then resulted in 67-year-old Des Thompson and 47-year-old Paul Heatley both dying in a hail of bullets.

At his trial the greying 57-year-old Earl Heatley displayed no regrets about his actions, and he refused to divulge any information about his drug contacts. He received a life imprisonment sentence at his fifth trial, but was released on the 7th April 2004.

Since then Heatley has continued to claim his innocence and is seeking compensation for being wrongly imprisoned for a decade.

CHOOSING YOUR FRIENDS AND RELATIVES

Francis James Carter turned to a loved one and family members for help after he bashed Phillip Clayton to death with a baseball bat. The unfortunate murder victim was attacked because he allegedly spoke to Carter's girlfriend at a barbecue.

The indignant "lady" in the incident, Carmel Eva Houghton, helped Carter cut off his drinking mate's fingers with a pair of bolt cutters, and it was the murderer's brother and brother-in-law who helped dispose of the body in a 44 gallon drum. The corpse was found a month later, and following a high speed car chase Carter was arrested and charged with numerous offences including murder and armed robbery.

In prison Carter confirmed his reputation as being the most dangerous man in Australia.

In prison Carter confirmed his reputation as being the most dangerous man in Australia. In January 1990 he stabbed fellow inmate Scott Wallace to death for allegedly disclosing confidential information to authorities, Carter was undeterred by the further life sentence he received for this murder, and in July 1991 he led a mass break out of eight prisoners from Queensland's Moreton Gaol. All were recaptured within days.

...in July 1991 he led a mass break out of eight prisoners from Queensland's Moreton Gaol.

Carter was 34 when he ended Phillip Clayton's life in a frenzy of rage, and this vicious man with a long criminal record had the reputation of being particularly dangerous when affected by alcohol. Carter is now serving a maximum security sentence and is unlikely to ever be released.

A DOMINANT FATHER

On 24th February 1988 the home that Christine Hicks shared with horse trainer and habitual criminal Allen Hall was burnt to the ground. The couple had recently begun a de facto relationship, and a written note stating "More is to come" accompanied the disaster. The couple were convinced that the culprit was Cec Waters.

Cec Waters was the father and trainer of three outstanding professional boxers. Guy and Troy Waters were Commonwealth champions and Dean Waters was the Australian heavy weight champion. On a June night in the year Christine Hick's house was destroyed, Guy Waters and his gym trainer Damon Cooper were hiding in the bushes when Allen Hall went outside his home to investigate the reason for his dogs barking. Shots rang out and Hall received fatal wounds.

Cec Waters

Cec Waters completely dominated the actions and thoughts of all his sons and Cooper. He and Hicks, who was 20 years his junior, were previously associated in a de facto relationship, but she left the bullying autocrat and took out an Aggravated Violence Order (AVO) against him before she set up house with Hall. Her bitter ex-lover told his son Dean that Hall and Hicks "had to die" and by 1 May 1988 two graves had been freshly dug in the Ourimbah State Forest.

On 29th June Dean Waters and Cooper succumbed to the demands of the tyrant. A 12 gauge shotgun and a .22 rifle ended Halls' life, but Cec chastised Dean for sparing the life of Hicks. Police discovered a footprint that appeared to match the tread of Dean Waters' runners, and incriminating car tyre marks were also found near the crime scene.

...two graves had been freshly dug in the Ourimbah State Forest.

Both Cooper and Dean Waters were first charged with conspiring to murder Hall, but two months later the charges against Dean Waters and Cooper were elevated to murder and Cec Waters was named as an accessory. However in July 1989 a magistrate dismissed all charges, stating that there was insufficient evidence to result in any convictions.

Psychiatric reports, which detailed the extent of Cec Waters' brutal domination over his son...

Nearly eight years later, on 8th February 1997, Dean Waters presented himself at nearby Wyong Police Station on the NSW Central Coast, and confessed to the 1988 murder of Allen Hall. Both he and Cooper were charged with murder and arson while Cec Waters was named as an accessory. The dominant father and employer denied all allegations, but he died from a heart attack before facing trial.

Dean Waters pleaded not guilty to murder on the grounds of diminished responsibility, but indicated that he was prepared to plead guilty to manslaughter. Psychiatric reports, which detailed the extent of Cec Waters' brutal domination over his son Dean, provided compelling evidence, and on 31st July 1997 Dean Waters was found not guilty on all charges.

His accomplice was not as fortunate. Damon Cooper was sentenced to a custodial sentence of 18 years with a non parole period of 12 years. A subsequent appeal by Cooper against the severity of his sentence was dismissed on 24th February 1998.

INFAMOUS BLOODLINES

Kath Pettingill

Kath Pettingill's nickname was "Granny Evil", and the former brothel madam gave birth to four criminal sons from three different partners. Suspected double murderer, drug trafficker and armed robber Victor Peirce was one notorious son, and his younger brother Lex Peirce also has a minor criminal record. Jamie Pettingill, a drug dealer and possible accomplice in the Walsh Street murders, was also spawned by "Granny Evil", but the most chilling offspring she produced was Dennis Allen.

Dennis Allen was strongly alleged to have committed two murders, but may have been responsible for as many as 12. He was a regular police informer who received support from strong elements in the Victorian force. This may explain why Allen was bailed over 60 times on often serious charges. The murderer and drug dealer became a wealthy property owner, and the many members of Melbourne's underworld whom he intimidated dubbed Dennis Allen "Mr. Death" or "Mr. D".

... many members of Melbourne's underworld whom he intimidated dubbed Dennis Allen "Mr. Death" or "Mr. D".

Allen's first serious brush with the law occurred in 1973, when he was imprisoned for rape. Before long, he was charged with possessing unlicensed weapons and harbouring an escapee (his half-brother Jamie Pettingill). By 1983 he was suspected of murdering close associate Greg

Pasche, and he may also have been implicated in the permanent disappearance of heroin addict Victor Gouroff.

No motive was obvious in 1984 when he allegedly murdered his friend Wayne Stanhope, who was shot several times in the head and had his throat cut. Allen's girlfriend and another couple were ordered to clean up the resultant mess, and three of Allen's brothers removed the corpse, before Stanhope's van was torched. The victim's body was never found.

...administered a lethal injection to prostitute Helga Wagnegg.

In September of that same year, Lindsay Simpson was shot dead in front of his family. This was apparently a case of mistaken identity, and the alleged real target was drug dealer Alan Williams. This contract killing was undertaken by NSW prison escapee Lindsay Pollitt, who was arrested and charged after Allen tipped off police.

Allen then perpetrated a 1984 homicide trifecta, when he allegedly administered a lethal injection to prostitute Helga Wagnegg. Again it was Allen who informed police about her November demise.

In March 1986 police received another murder tip off, and it was the dismembered body of Hells Angels biker Anton Kenny that was found inside a 44 gallon drum in the Yarra River. The corpse was riddled with 5.32 calibre bullets, and Kenny's legs had been removed. They were later found encased in concrete.

Allen named Peter Ian Robertson as the killer, and he was duly charged. Robertson admitted he was present in the house when the murder took place, but claimed that Allen shot and later sawed up the dead body. This grizzly process was interrupted at times when Allen joined other guests at a nearby party.

...chased his wife Wendy around the house while he waved some of Kenny's amputated body parts at her.

"Mr D" was apparently in a jovial mood during the amputation. Half-brother Victor Peirce was invited to partly witness the occasion, and Peirce allegedly chased his wife Wendy around the house while he waved some of Kenny's amputated body parts at her. Violent behaviour has been an integral part of Wendy Peirce's life for many years, but this gross act was too extreme by anyone's standards.

Soon after, Allen's close ties with police again rescued him after he was arrested for assaulting a neighbour. Bail was granted almost immediately after the court was told that Dennis Allen was assisting police in a murder inquiry.

However by 1986 Allen's rare heart condition was taking toll on his health, and witnesses to his past grotesque deeds began to come forward. The files of Gouroff, Wagnegg, Simpson and Stanhope were re-opened, and Allen's girlfriend confessed that the original evidence she submitted about Anton Kenny was untrue.

After Allen left hospital on 11th March 1987, he was arrested and charged with Stanhope's murder, but died in April before the case went to court. His mother Kath Pettingill later claimed that Allen admitted his guilt about the Kenny murder in a death bed confession.

The life of a much feared man is over. However, the power of Dennis Allen to enforce silence, only ended when he himself faced the same death penalty that he inflicted on his many victims.

CHAPTER TEN:

BIKIE GANGS ACROSS AUSTRALIA

THE TOWN THE GYPSIES CURSED

Don Hancock was known as the "The Silver Fox" by admiring Western Australian police colleagues. In 1982 Hancock supposedly solved Australia's largest gold theft, when he arrested the three Mickleberg brothers for stealing 65 kilograms of the precious metal. It was alleged that he resorted to brutal interrogation tactics to gain the confessions he needed, but Don Hancock ended his legendary policing career as the Commander of the Criminal Investigation Branch (CIB).

In retirement, his wife Elizabeth and he moved to the small Central Goldfields hamlet of Ora Banda- a town that was virtually the domain of the Hancock family. They owned the Ora Banda Historic Inn, which incorporated a pub, beer garden and restaurant. They also owned three houses, some single men's quarters and a diesel gold crusher. The town's trailer park, general store, seven motel units and the gold lease on Grant's Patch, were all owned by the Hancocks.

October 1st 2000 commenced a popular holiday weekend in Ora Banda, but "the Silver Fox" scented trouble when a group of Gypsy Jokers joined the other tourists. By reputation "the Jokers" were the most violent of all Australian bike gangs, and their members profited greatly from both illegal and legal business interests.

..."criminal scumbags" began to drink heavily and roared around the track on their motor bikes.

After arriving noisily in town, the bikies took over the race track area, which Don Hancock had earmarked for community sporting activities. The Gypsy Joker banner was attached between trees, and Hancock seethed when the "criminal scumbags" began to drink heavily and roared around the track on their motor bikes.

By the end of the day the Jokers gravitated to the centre of town, where gang member James "Spud" Manson insulted a local prospector. Then Hancock's daughter Alison received some mild but unwanted verbal sexual abuse from "Billy" Grierson, which drew an irate response from her father. When the argument began to escalate Hancock closed down the pub, and he then furiously drove his utility towards Grant's Patch where he reportedly stored a gun.

The bikies moved back to their camping area, and by 6.50 pm they were relaxing outdoors and drinking their own supplies of alcohol. An hour later a shot rang out, and the Jokers hurriedly took cover. They resumed socialising when the situation appeared to normalise, but ten minutes later another shot punctured the air, and the huge form of "Billy" Grierson slumped to the ground.

...another shot punctured the air, and the huge form of "Billy" Grierson slumped to the ground.

The seriously wounded bikie was rushed to a first aid station but was soon pronounced dead. His hooded denim vest, with the Gypsy Jokers' patch of iron cross and swastika, was stripped from his body. The revengeful group then returned to Ora Banda, to search for "the white haired bloke we had trouble with this arvo".

By then about 40 people were still in town, and all of them presented credible alibis to investigators. Don Hancock was spotted around 9 pm in the beer garden, but he refused to speak to police without legal advice. Senior Constable Dave Roper ordered him to remain at the inn for further questioning, but "The Silver Fox" slipped away to his own "lair", where he changed his clothes and had a shower.

Two constables soon visited the Hancock home, where they found Don Hancock eating an orange, the citric acid of which reputedly disguises gunshot residue. He accompanied the

...angry declaration being shouted at the police escort as they left.

police back to the inn, from where he telephoned his lawyer in Perth. By then Detective Senior Sergeant Kim Gage from Kalgoorlie, the officer in charge of the case, was placed in an invidious position, as he had socialised with Hancock earlier that day.

Hancock's firearms were confiscated, but both his wife and he still refused to provide statements to police. Gage decided that he didn't have enough evidence to issue a search warrant; a grave error which outraged the bikies.

Two constables guarded the crime scene for the rest of the night, and the remaining police returned to Kalgoorlie. Next morning, around 11 am, the Hancocks returned to Perth in a police patrol car, with this angry declaration being shouted at the police escort as they left Ora Banda.

"F… you and your ways!" shouted Gypsy Jokers' leader Graeme "Slim" Slater, "I'm going to take care of it my way".

CIB detective Jack Lee soon arrived at Ora Banda, and immediately removed Gage from the case because of his conflict of interest. Lee suspected that Hancock was the shooting culprit, but realised that missed opportunities early in the investigation hindered the chance of a conviction. The weapon used in the killing was not found.

The bikies apparently left the area after Grierson was buried at Kalgoolie on October 13th, but that night, just as Ora Banda was slipping back into its customary state of lethargy, the opening blast of the Bikies' revenge erupted.

The historic inn was virtually razed from the earth by a gigantic explosion. Gypsy Joker leaders Slater and Sid "Snot" Reid were soon rounded up and questioned about the bombing, but both had watertight alibis.

Destructive mayhem in "Billy's resting place" continued. Hancock's Ora Banda house was unsuccessfully bombed on 1st November, but four days later three dangerously effective home made bombs ripped apart a house, the mill and the hotel. Ora Banda no longer existed-it had virtually been blown away.

Ora Banda no longer existed-it had virtually been blown away.

The Jokers then began the final uncompromising phase of their vendetta – the planned execution of Don Hancock. Slater and Reid became patched members of the Gypsy Joker club in Perth. Then, through a government contact, they discovered the address of Lou Lewis, an ex-bookmaker friend of Hancock's. They had discovered that Lewis often drove Hancock to Saturday horse race meetings, and they began to target the pair.

Police had feared for the Hancock's safety, since they re-located to Perth. Video surveillance was unsuccessfully trialed, but the couples' reluctance to co-operate with security safeguards, or change their routines, thwarted police efforts. After a Gypsy Joker member was spotted near the Hancock home, "The Silver Fox" was urged to escape to a safe haven in New Zealand, but this advice also went unheeded. Meanwhile investigations into the Grierson death had stalled, though Lee successfully moved for a coronial hearing for 1st October 2001.

The explosion was heard kilometres away, and the car became a massive fireball.

A month before then, Lewis and Hancock followed their usual routine of attending the Saturday races in Perth. Their journey was closely monitored by Slater and Reid, and the dangerous duo was able to park their vehicle next to Lewis' 1981 Holden Commodore station wagon. Slater and Reid allegedly wired a gelignite bomb into the car, and after the race meeting ended, they trailed the two unsuspecting friends back to Hancock's home area.

"Rest in peace Billy", was the reported comment, when Slater allegedly activated the bomb with his cell phone. A huge explosion rocked the middle class neighbourhood where the two friends lived. The explosion was heard kilometres away, and the car became a massive fireball. The blast ripped Hancock's torso from his lower body, and landed near his swimming pool. Various other body organs of the two victims were later discovered in different parts of the neighbourhood.

"You were taken from us by a cowardly dog but remember buddy, every dog has its day."

Following the atrocity, Police Operation Zircon swung into action. A loaded, unlicensed pistol was found in Reid's house, as well as a photograph of the deceased Grierson, with the following inscription.

"Hey buddy, what to say? You were taken from us by a cowardly dog but remember buddy, every dog has its day."

Chapter president of the local Gypsy Jokers' club, Lenny Kirby, was arrested after a large supply of drugs and money was found at his property, but the bikies' code of silence prevailed and there was insufficient evidence for conviction.

For six months police exhaustively targeted Reid, and finally he agreed to help if both his girlfriend and he were protected. When he was satisfied with their assurances, Reid confessed to Hancock's murder.

Gary White, another Gypsy Joker, was convicted on another murder from Reid's information, but his evidence about Slater kept changing. Skilled QC Colin Lovett made much of this in court on Slater's behalf, and he also revealed double standards operating in the flimsy evidence provided by police. At the conclusion of the eight-week trial, Graeme Slater was acquitted on most charges.

Slater did serve two years in custody for bombing Hancock's Ora Banda house, but Detective Lee still fears that the hard evidence needed to convict the murderers of Hancock and Lewis, is yet to be revealed.

ANGELS FROM HELL

"Yea, though I walk through the valley of death I will fear no evil, because I am he the evilest mother f..... who ever walked through the valley."

These intimidating words are attributed to Peter John Hill, a founding member of the Hells Angels Club that formed in 1972. Hill came from an affluent family that educated him at a prestigious private school. He brought excellent management and business skills to the group, which became a dominant business force in Australian crime circles. Money was wisely invested in property, and the Angels also promoted rock concerts.

Hill introduced amphetamines (commonly known as speed) into Australia.

Hill introduced amphetamines (commonly known as speed) into Australia. He learned the manufacturing skills of this illegal substance, when he embraced the U.S outlaw sub culture during a trip to America in the late 1970s. Feared

Californian crime identities such as James "Jim Jim" Brandes, Sergei "Sir Gay" Walton, Kenny "KO" Owen and Sonny Barger, influenced Hill's education in drug manufacturing. It was Walton, however, who presented the Australian with the jackpot that he craved.

When Hill visited Walton in his Californian gaol, he was orally provided with the exact details he needed for the successful manufacture of speed. Hill hurriedly recorded this priceless information on three separate pieces of paper. After he returned to Australia, he repaid Walton by shipping back supplies of a chemical that was banned in America.

Hill wasted no time in profiting from "the keys to the kingdom". With administrative and technical assistance from fellow Hells Angels in Ray Hammett, John Maddon and Roger "Root Rat" Biddlestone, Hill began manufacturing speed. Their initial capital outlay was $15,000, which they raised by selling stolen motorbikes.

The Angels speed empire soon became a spectacular success. Money gained from the distribution of the drug was deposited with the Melbourne chapter of the club, and from there it was mostly invested in the property market.

The Angels speed empire soon became a spectacular success.

Belgrave was where the drug was first manufactured, but the group later moved their illegal operations to the less populated area of Wattle Glen, where the pungent processing smells were not as noticeable to the general public. From their semi-rural base the Angels transported speed in powder form all across the country, and profits of $70,000-$80,000 a day were not uncommon. Ominous signs were looming for the future however – many of the Angels were themselves becoming drug users

...profits of $70,000-$80,000 a day were not uncommon...

Soon after a smaller speed operation was opened up in Ballarat, disturbing news reached Bob Armstrong, a respected police officer who had pursued Peter Hill for many years. Hills' mother Audrey had long disapproved of her son's activities, and she informed Armstrong, that Peter was hiring an American "hitman" on a contract killing mission. The contract target for the feared "Jim Jim" Brandes was the "Benny Hill" look alike – Bob Armstrong.

The resolute detective adopted a defiant stance to the problem. When Brandes first arrived at Tullamarine airport on 26th August 1982, he was immediately placed in a holding cell. The flustered American then met the English comedian look alike that he had been hired to kill, and Armstrong informed him that his visa was cancelled. Brandes' convictions in USA for gun running and drug dealing caused him to be deemed an illegal immigrant, so the astonished contract killer soon found himself flying back to America.

By then the initial success of the Angels' speed empire had begun to falter. After John Maddon was killed in a motor bike accident, and Ray Hammett was caught stealing proceeds, Hill and Biddlestone became more isolated from the other Angels. The decline of the operation continued when the Ballarat laboratory was forced to close down, and Hill and his wife went into hiding.

More Hells Angels were now facing legal proceedings, and juries were often faced with stony stares from a formidable front row group of Hells Angels when evidence was submitted in court. One juror, Hill later revealed, was presented with a suitcase of money, and that case unsurprisingly resulted in a hung jury.

One juror, was presented with a suitcase of money, and that case unsurprisingly resulted in a hung jury.

Hill himself saw that the early glory days had ended after Biddlestone was badly beaten by fellow Angels, and the drug empires founder testified against fellow bikies. Biddleston, who was possibly intimidated by his former comrades, refused to give evidence, so the case collapsed.

After spending five years in custody, Hill and his family moved to an isolated rural area where he grew oranges and drove trucks for a living. It is alleged that he sold his speed recipes to the Black Ohlans bike gang for the astonishingly low fee of $1,000.

For the next 15 years, the speed empire came under the leadership of the notorious John Higgs, a ruthless man who subsequently paid contract killer James Frederick Bazley to eliminate drug couriers Doug and Isobel Wilson. Higgs became the country's main distributor, but he was later gaoled for six years after undercover police helped discover his illegal operations. When the arrest was made in 1994, John Higgs was allegedly in possession of $4,000,000 worth of equipment and chemicals.

In recent years, rival bikie gangs have engaged in violent battles for control of the speed empire. Over 30 people died in a five-year gang war period, and Bob Armstrong withdrew from police anti-drug operational teams in an effort to protect his undercover agents. Arrests have been forthcoming, but many of them have been for minor offences.

CHAPTER ELEVEN:

PROGRAMMED TO KILL

BRIEF PROFILE OF SERIAL KILLERS

Serial killers tend to be white males, of average intelligence, and from middle class backgrounds. In childhood they are often subject to abuse, and during these years they tend to torture domestic animals.

Potential perpetrators do not relate well to other people. Usually they target a particular group to kill, such as children, homosexuals or prostitutes. They are likely to hoard items of clothing, ornaments or body parts of the victims as trophies. Serial killers are also likely to return to the crime scene, either as spectators or participants.

Pre-crime stressors that activate homicides can either be of major or minor significance. Guns are rarely used in the killings; poisonings, strangulations or stabbings are all more prevalent means of extermination.

William MacDonald

Such predators are experts in rationalising their chilling crimes, as they seldom accept personal responsibility for the carnage they have caused.

MUTILATION KILLINGS OF THE 1960S

The obvious homosexual traits of William MacDonald made him the subject of ridicule and bashings from fellow servicemen, when he served in the British army during the 1940s. He blamed an abusive relationship with an officer for the sexual preferences he developed, and in 1947 MacDonald was so distressed by his violent fantasies that he voluntarily entered a mental institution.

MacDonald was so distressed by his violent fantasies that he voluntarily entered a mental institution.

MacDonald came to Australia as an immigrant in 1955, and by 1960 a series of murders occurred in Brisbane and Sydney. On 4th June, 55-year-old Amos Hurst was slain. This was followed by a frenzied attack in November 1961 on 45-year-old Alfred Greenfield, when 30 knife wounds were inflicted to the Sydney victim.. The 31st March 1962 saw the homicide of 65-year-old Ernest Cobbin, and there were gruesome similarities about all these brutal murders. Every victim was a derelict, and all had their testicles and penises savagely hacked off with a knife.

A huge police hunt began just when MacDonald was experiencing personal problems. He had no home after falling out with his landlady, and he was sacked from his employment with the Post Master Generals' Department (PMG). In an effort to make a new start, MacDonald assumed the name of Alan Edward Brennan, and opened up a mixed business in the Sydney suburb of Burwood.

...came as a shock six months later when he bumped into his "deceased" friend...

The murder of homeless men resumed when 42-year-old James Hackett, a former inmate of Long Bay Prison, was killed by MacDonald in his home above the shop. The body and blood stained clothes were buried underneath the building, and under the alias of Alan MacDonald the murderer moved back to Brisbane.

Three weeks later, a decomposing corpse was discovered at the shop site, and it was assumed that the deceased man was "Alan Edward Brennan" who was similar in age and appearance. Police did not suspect foul play, but the investigating coroner expressed misgivings. The shirt of the deceased had knife slashes, and there were blood stains on the shop floor and on the bedroom mattress.

John McCarthy, a former acquaintance of "Brennan", attended his funeral, and it came as a shock six months later when he bumped into his "deceased" friend in busy George Street in Sydney. After being queried by a curious McCarthy when they shared a few drinks, a worried MacDonald hurriedly packed some possessions and moved to Melbourne.

At first police were sceptical when McCarthy claimed that he had been socialising with a "walking corpse", but he soon convinced journalists from Sydney's "Daily Mirror" that his story was authentic. The resulting publicity caused the body of "Brennan" to be exhumed, and a finger print examination revealed that the corpse was Hackett. The search for the mutilation killer then focussed on the whereabouts of William MacDonald.

By then, under another assumed name, the wanted man had been employed for three days by the Victorian Railways in Melbourne's CBD. Some of his young workmates noted MacDonald's distinctive Liverpudlian accent, and the likeness of him to photographs being featured in newspapers. The end was near for the mutilation murderer.

After his arrest, MacDonald pleaded not guilty to four murders on the grounds of insanity, and claimed he saw his former army officer tormentor in every victim he killed. Phantom voices, MacDonald asserted, urged him to kill prior to these murderous attacks.

Phantom voices, MacDonald asserted, urged him to kill prior to these murderous attacks.

Macdonald's submissions were disregarded, and he was sentenced to life imprisonment. In custody he attempted to strangle a fellow inmate, and languished for the rest of his life in high security prisons for the criminally insane.

Peter Dupas

CAUGHT IN THE MIDDLE

Police knew that Peter Dupas (already convicted of two homicides and was the prime suspect in two other unsolved killings) had also ended the life of Mersina Halvagis at Melbourne's Fawkner Cemetery in 2002. The frustrating reality, however, was that vital primary evidence necessary for a conviction had not come to light. When the crucial breakthrough finally surfaced, it came from an unexpected source.

Peter Dupas was a monster in Victorian communities for over 20 years. In 1968, when he was a 15-year-old schoolboy, Dupas attacked a 27-year-old female neighbour with a knife. Rehabilitation proved to be a fruitless task, and over the years short intervals of freedom was inevitably followed by several gaol terms for rape, false imprisonment and finally two counts of murder.

Peter Dupas was a monster in Victorian communities for over 20 years.

The 1997 killing of 40-year-old prostitute Margaret Maher, began a disturbing pattern to the bestial homicides of Peter Dupas. The body was horribly mutilated, and the woman's breasts had been completely severed and stuffed in her mouth.

Nicole Patterson

At that time the murderer remained undetected, but an arrest came three days after Dupas murdered 29-year-old psychiatrist Nicole Patterson on March 19th, 1999. Again the breasts of the victim were removed, and Patterson received 27 stab wounds in the frenzied attack that occurred in her own home. On 15th August 2000, Peter Dupas was sentenced to life imprisonment without parole.

...received 27 stab wounds in the frenzied attack that occurred in her own home.

The inconspicuous and socially inept Dupas, remained a strong suspect in the unsolved Mersina Halvagis homicide case. This young woman had been attending to her grandmother's grave before she was savagely attacked, and the mutilations suffered were similar to those experienced a month before to Margaret Maher. In that case DNA samples were vital in the successful conviction of Dupas, but no such primary evidence was available to the prosecution lawyers before the trial of Peter Dupas began in 2007.

As the court case loomed closer, a desperate investigating detective directed his attention to inmates who had shared custodial sentences with the serial killer in Melbourne's Port Phillip Prison. He discovered that one particular prisoner had worked and socialised quite frequently with the taciturn Dupas. That prisoner was Andrew Fraser.

For years prior to his fall from grace, Andrew

Fraser had been a brilliant defence barrister for various well known business entrepreneurs and underworld figures. Alan Bond, Dennis Allen, the Moran family and the five men accused of the Walsh Street murders, had all benefited from the advice and clever courtroom tactics of Fraser. In contrast he became a hated figure in police circles, especially among those who experienced his biting sarcasm in cross examinations in court.

...he became a hated figure in police circles (due to his) biting sarcasm in cross examinations in court.

Fraser, however, became a cocaine addict. His opulent and decadent lifestyle began to falter, as his addiction became more serious, and Andrew Fraser received a five year sentence after being found guilty of cocaine trafficking

To some the sentence seemed unduly harsh, especially when the "white collar" criminal's sentence began in the maximum security area of Port Philip Prison. There Fraser was confined with dangerous psychopaths such as Raymond Edmunds, Les Camilleri and Peter Dupas.

Dupas and Fraser often worked together in the prison gardens, and after Fraser was transferred to a minimum security gaol near Sale, a detective assigned to the Halvagis case contacted him before Peter Dupas faced trial for the murder of the young woman. The detective travelled to the Gippsland prison to interview Fraser, and their conversation was very fruitful.

Fraser revealed to the detective, and later to the jury at the murder trial, that Dupas not only admitted to him that he killed the young woman; he also re-enacted how he stabbed a kneeling Halvagis when he attacked her at the cemetery. At that stage, police had not divulged that the woman was in a kneeling position when she was murdered, so the careless revelation of the killer became very damaging.

...he also re-enacted how he stabbed a kneeling Halvagis when he attacked her at the cemetery.

Peter Dupas was found guilty of murdering Mersina Halvagis, and he received a further life sentence that will be served concurrently with the other life sentences. He is unlikely to ever be released from custody.

Fraser is now free again. He has written a book called "Court In The Middle", which is highly critical of the prison system. The former legal "high flyer" now enjoys an almost anonymous existence on a rural property, which is very different to the affluent and influential life style he once knew.

SERIAL KILLER AT TYNONG NORTH

During the early 1980s, the bodies of three women aged between 15 and 75 were found in dense scrub near Pakenham to the south-east of Melbourne.

The victims were 15-year-old Catherine

Linda Headland from Berwick, 19-year-old Ann-Marie Sargeant from Cranbourne and 75-year-old Bertha Miller, a relative of Mick Miller, the former Victorian Police Commissioner. The remains of the deceased women were found near Brew Road in Tynong North, and, despite intensive investigations, no-one has currently been charged with the murders.

The remains of the deceased women were found near Brew Road in Tynong North...

Well after the killings ceased, Senior Sergeant Clive Rust announced that "police do believe they have identified the offender responsible for these murders". He then described the suspect as being 68 years of age, who was a married man with children. Additional information revealed that the man had strong church ties, he had past contacts with police, and he worked as a projectionist at the time of the killings.

The Melbourne major daily newspapers eagerly added further information. "The Age" provided a written description of the man in question, and two days later the "Sun-Herald" was even more revealing in its information about the prime suspect. He was actually named, and his photograph appeared in the state's most widely read newspaper.

Harold Janman, the subject of these speculations, protested his innocence, and questions were raised about the premature and invasive revelations that had been made public, about a person who had not been charged. "Herald Sun" editor Peter Blunden defended his paper's coverage of the investigation, and stated his belief that the information revealed would not prejudice any future trial.

The outcome has been that Janman, who allegedly failed lie detection tests about two of the victims, has never been charged with the murders. Police believe that the murderer stopped re-offending after the bodies were discovered over 20 years ago, and the case is still under review.

CHAOS IN CLAREMONT

"God has gone into our garden, and picked the most beautiful rose".

"God has gone into our garden, and picked the most beautiful rose".

These poignant words formed part of the funeral eulogy that Dennis Glennon presented about his 27-year-old daughter Ciara. She was one of three women who were murdered in a series of unsolved killings around the Perth suburb of Claremont between 1996-97.

The body of one of the victims has never been located, there were no eye witnesses when each of the three women vanished, and there was no apparent motive for the homicides.

Eighteen-year-old Sandra Spiers was the first victim to vanish. The young woman reportedly consumed generous amounts of alcohol in the Claremont nightclub area on 27th January 1996, before ringing a taxi in the early hours of the morning. However no client was waiting for the driver at the designated pick-up area, so he left the busy nightclub strip to collect other passengers celebrating the Australia Day weekend.

The Spiers family reported that their daughter was missing next day, but the police treated the situation as a mundane missing person's case that would soon be resolved. No further action was taken for two more crucial weeks, and Sandra Spiers has never been found.

On 9th June of that same year a possibly drink affected Jane Rimmer also disappeared in the same Claremont nightclub strip. She was reported missing by her family the following night, and on this occasion police reacted quickly. Various suspects were exhaustively questioned, but no arrests resulted.

...Rimmer also disappeared in the same Claremont nightclub strip.

Nearly eight weeks later, on a cold August day, the badly decomposed body of Jane Rimmer was found near a road in rural Wellard, 40 kilometres south of Perth. The young woman was naked, her clothing and handbag were missing, but she had not apparently been sexually assaulted. Police noted that she was similar in appearance to Spiers, and both young women had been educated at the

...on a cold August day, the badly decomposed body of Jane Rimmer was found near a road...

same school. "Rogue" taxi drivers became especially targeted by police at that time, and around 80 of them lost their jobs for various reasons.

Nine months later, on 14th March, 1997, Ciara Glennon was sharing social drinks with her boss Neil Fearis at Claremont's Continental Hotel. Fearis departed around 11 pm, and shortly afterwards Glennon left the premises from an unknown exit. Fearis was later cleared of any suspicion, and after Glennon vanished the Western Australian Government offered a $50,000 reward for any information about the three missing women.

In early April the body of Ciara Glennon was found at Eglinton near Yanchep, 40 kilometres from Perth. The two discovered bodies of Rimmer and Glennon were 86 kilometres apart, but only about 50 kilometres from the city's CBD.

Police intensified their investigations, and by September 1997 they regularly observed a white Hyundai sedan trawling the Claremont nightclub area between midnight and 2 am. It appeared that young women were being stalked. A license check indicated that the registered driver was 41-year-old Lance Kenneth Williams.

After identifying the suspect, a police woman decoy was positioned to be picked up by Williams, before later being safely dropped off at her destination. No advances of any kind were made, and Williams seemed more interested in talking about himself in a boring monotone voice.

Ciara Glennon

Early on April 5th 1998, a police tactical response team pulled the trawling Hyundai off the road. Williams was apprehended at gunpoint, and the shaken man lost control of his bladder during the sudden arrest. He was subjected to several hours of intense interrogation, but remained calm and did not seek legal representation.

It appeared that young women were being stalked.

After consistently maintaining his innocence during a gruelling period of questioning, Lance Williams was finally released without charge. Later his car, his unit and his parents' home were exhaustively searched, but no incriminating evidence was found.

Police probing revealed that Williams was regarded as "Mr. Average". He is of average height and build, and is the oldest of five children. In his schooldays he was remembered as being an intelligent student who was especially good at Mathematics. Socially, however, Williams has always been a "loner" who avoids eye contact in conversations. Julie Cutler, who vanished near Cottesloe Beach in 1998, was one of his school peers, and following the Claremont murders Lance Williams was closely questioned about her disappearance.

At the age of 14 he suffered severe concussion. On leaving school Williams worked as a bank teller between the ages of 17-28, and as a 23-year-old he attempted to commit suicide after suffering his first nervous breakdown. Many years before, it was recalled he once escorted a girl to a cinema, but it is unlikely that he has ever been involved in a meaningful relationship with the opposite sex. Police discovered that in his adult years he has visited prostitutes, but has only sought hand masturbation as a service.

...as a 23-year-old he attempted to commit suicide after suffering his first nervous breakdown.

Domestically Williams alternates between living at the family home and caring for himself in a unit. He reveals a strong degree of self-control. In the past he was a heavy drinker, smoker and gambler, but now completely abstains from these indulgences.

When the media scrutiny on Williams' activities was at its most intense, he twice voluntarily undertook a polygraph or lie detection test, which he failed on both occasions. It is rumoured that this middle-aged bachelor can, with little provocation, have sudden fits of intense anger.

The other prime suspect in the case is completely different in his personality and lifestyle. Peter Waygers, who was Mayor of Claremont between 1995-1997, was President of the Western Australian Council for Civil Liberties when he was questioned at length by police after Jane Rimmer disappeared.

The big, extroverted man had the reputation of making inappropriate remarks to women, and he had no alibi for the night Rimmer was murdered. Search warrants were issued for further investigations into the Claremont murders, but no further action resulted. Ironically Waygers later became the first civil libertarian to champion Lance Williams' rights against harassment from police, and he stated his fear that the Williams could be driven to commit suicide.

The big, extroverted man had the reputation of making inappropriate remarks to women...

Police pressure on the former mayor continued. On 5th September 2004, plain clothed officers, accompanied by a strong media presence, swooped on Wayger's home. No criminal evidence was found, but ten days later he was asked to provide a DNA sample. No reason for this drastic step was provided, and during that time Waygers was allegedly forbidden to answer his home telephone, while his computer was confiscated.

Two weeks later the Claremont Council office premises were searched. Again no explanation was forthcoming about why such measures were warranted.

The guilt or innocence of Lance Williams, and to a lesser extent Peter Waygers, was much debated at the time.

But the Macro Task Force specifically set up to investigate the Claremont killings had a "Eureka" moment in January 2009. Forensic DNA evidence taken from Ciara Glennon's body and sent to the UK for analysis via a technique not available in Australia uncovered DNA from an unknown man. Eight years later, police identified their suspect – Telstra technician Bradley Robert Edwards. Edwards was tried and convicted of the murders of Ciara Glennon and Jane Rimmer and in December 2020 sentenced to life behind bars.

There was not enough evidence to convict him of the murder of Sarah Spiers, however the presiding judge noted that Edwards was her likely killer. Almost a quarter of a century after the murders, a story that shocked and tortured Perth, and 3 families in particular, was finally laid to rest.

CHAPTER TWELVE:

OVER THE WALL

ALIGHTING FROM A TRAM

Darcy Ezekiel Dugan, who died in 1991 at the age of 71, is arguably the most notorious escape artist and armed robber that NSW has ever known.

Dugan, who once even robbed a hospital office at gunpoint, is best remembered for the brazen escape he made from a prison tram in 1947. The tram was transporting prisoners on a short journey from Darlinghurst Courthouse to Long Bay Gaol, when Dugan made his escape by cutting a hole through the tram roof with a kitchen knife he had procured.

After one of his many escapes Darcy Dugan scrawled a cheeky note on his cell wall which read "gone to Gowings", (then a popular Sydney department store).

OLD BILL

"Old Bill" also spent 14 years in solitary confinement; a soul destroying punishment when he never saw the sun.

William James O' Meally was a tough gaol veteran who became Victoria's longest serving prisoner. He was initially sentenced to death after being found guilty of the shooting murder of Constable George Howell on 30th January 1952. His death sentence was finally reprieved, but O'Meally became the last prisoner in custody to receive a legal flogging.

This harsh penalty was carried out in 1957 after a police officer was shot in the thigh when O'Meally and Robert Henry Taylor unsuccessfully attempted to escape from Pentridge Gaol. Their taste of freedom only lasted 13 minutes, for O'Meally received 12 lashes. "Old Bill" also spent 14 years in solitary confinement; a soul destroying punishment when he never saw the sun.

It has to be said that "Old Bill" was not a successful escape artist. In a 1965 attempt to "go over the wall", he was arrested only 200 metres from the prison walls.

During his long period in custody O'Meally embraced Christianity, and he also penned many stories, poems and plays. A child was born to his wife when he first faced trial in 1952, and after O'Meally was finally released 27 years later, he met both his son and grandchild for the very first time.

"Old Bill" always maintained that he did not kill the police constable, and 16 years after he was freed the physically frail 75-year-old unsuccessfully attempted to have his case re-opened.

HIS OWN FAN CLUB

In late 1959 Kevin Simmonds and Leslie Newcombe escaped from Sydney's Long Bay Gaol through a ventilation duct in the prison chapel. When a massive man hunt commenced in the next 24 hours, the pair spent their first night of freedom huddled close together in a freshly dug grave at Botany Cemetery.

Two days later, the desperate pair broke into Emu Plains Prison Farm in an attempt to steal needed supplies. During the break in, they were discovered by a prison warden, who they brutally beaten to death with a cricket stump and baseball bat.

The search for the duo intensified, and Newcombe was arrested within a fortnight. Simmons continued to elude capture, and during his 37 days on the run the handsome escapee from the NSW Riverina town of Griffith, became a cult hero to some impressionable people in the community.

A Sydney schoolgirl started a "Kevin Simmonds fan club", and a group of housewives

...escaped from Sydney's Long Bay Gaol through a ventilation duct in the prison chapel.

declared that they would provide him with a hot meal if the chance arose. No hot meal or fan club members were on hand when Simmons was arrested in the NSW coastal town of Kurri Kurri.

No hot meal or fan club members were on hand when Simmons was arrested in the NSW coastal town of Kurri Kurri.

Both Simmons and Newcombe initially faced murder charges, but in a surprising twist the charges were changed to manslaughter, which, in the words of the judge "was the worst case (of manslaughter) I have ever known." Both were found guilty, and received life imprisonment terms.

Much of their sentence was served in Grafton Gaol, which was then known as "the Alcatraz of Australian gaols." Biographies written since by Newcombe and Simmonds' sister, detail the brutal treatment that both men routinely received, and Kevin Simmonds committed suicide within Grafton Gaol in 1986.

GLOBAL CELEBRITY

Ronald Arthur Biggs became a famous fugitive in Britain, Australia, Brazil and Barbados, before he voluntarily returned to his native England, where he passed away in December 2013. Ronnie Biggs' daring escapes, his almost legendary ability to avoid capture, and the support provided by his friends and various lovers, converted a petty criminal into an international celebrity. His path to global notoriety began with the Great Train Robbery in England on 8th August, 1963.

A young Ronald Briggs

At the time this robbery was the most lucrative ever perpetrated in Britain, and it was planned with military type precision by Bruce Reynolds, who was the chief organiser. The thieves even had mock army vehicles, and during the robbery they communicated with walkie-talkies. A massive three million pounds was stolen in the raid, which is approximately the equivalent of A$120,000,000–130,000,000 in today's values.

It was the Glasgow to London mail train that transported this treasure trove of wealth to where the raid began 30 miles from London at Sears Crossing in Buckinghamshire. At Sear's Crossing, a red signal light unexpectedly brought the train to a halt. Jack Mills, the driver, noticed that the light was green beyond the crossing, and he suspected that an electrical fault had occurred. His fireman, David Whitby, was sent on by foot to investigate.

Ronnie Biggs' daring escapes, his almost legendary ability to avoid capture, converted a petty criminal into an international celebrity.

Whitby soon noticed that the nearby phone link had been severed, and before long he was surrounded by a mob of hooded men. The terrified fireman was not hurt by the thugs, but after they swarmed onto the stationery train Jack Mills received a serious head injury, from which he never recovered.

All the unwanted train coaches were then uncoupled by the gang, so that the engine and its precious cargo could be moved to a more convenient unloading site. During the operation, all but one of the gang avoided conversation. The gregarious exception was later identified by witnesses as being Ronnie Biggs.

It was Biggs who had been allocated the role of enticing a former train driver to join them so that the engine could be moved on, but he failed dismally in this mission. The mechanism of the modern train was far beyond the old recruit's experience, so the impatient robbers forced the badly injured Jack Mills to move the train to their unloading destination.

...Ronnie's prints were found on a monopoly set and a sauce bottle at the farm.

The gang then hid away for several days at Leathersdale Farm while they counted their ill gotten gains and shared out the proceeds, before they began to disperse. "Cleaners" were given the task of removing all traces of fingerprints from the location, and a "dustman" was also hired to burn down the farmhouse.

Biggs left the scene with Bruce Reynolds, who had masterminded the operation. Later Ronnie and his wife Charmain gleefully counted his share of the proceeds, which amounted to the handsome sum of approximately A$6,000,000.

The strategies for escape were both daring and ambitious.

Their gloating, however, was short lived, as Ronnie's prints were found on a monopoly set and a sauce bottle at the farm. He and several others were soon arrested and sent to trial. Ironically, the failed engine driver was one of three gang members who were never apprehended.

The first court case on 20th January 1964 was declared a mistrial. However on 28th March the sentences handed down to all the captured perpetrators were harsh, and. Biggs was sentenced to a formidable 30 years in custody.

He was soon transported to Wandsworth Prison where security was considered to be tight. Biggs' spirits lifted when Charlie Wilson, one of his partners in crime, successfully escaped from Birmingham Gaol. Wilson finally re-located to Canada, where he evaded the law for over three years before being arrested by "the Mounties", (the Royal Canadian Mounted Police).

Biggs began to hatch his own escape plans, and during compulsory exercise sessions he ingratiated himself with other inmates to aid his dash for freedom. One he confided in was the soon to be released Paul Seabourne, and it was he who later secured the outside arrangements. The strategies for escape were both daring and ambitious.

It was decided that a high roofed furniture van would park next to the 25 feet high exterior prison wall at a designated time and date. A rostrum five feet in height would then be levered up from the open van to the top of the wall, and Seabourne and other masked men would lower rope ladders down into the prison exercise yard.

Biggs, together with any other would-be escapees, would then take advantage of a planned diversion, (that would hopefully require the immediate attention of unsuspecting wardens), and clamber up the ladders to the top of the wall. From there they would jump down through the roof of the van onto a pile of mattresses, and be driven to freedom.

...the pair also undertook expensive and painful plastic surgery to alter their facial appearances.

Against all odds the plan worked to perfection, and both Biggs and the convicted armed robber Eric Flowers successfully made their way to a "safe house". The celebrity fame of Ronnie Biggs had begun, and an embarrassed British Government actively encouraged the police force to quickly hunt down the glamorised fugitives. Biggs and Flowers kept on the move, shifting first to London's East End, and then Camberwell, before sailing on to France.

There Flowers became "Bob Burley", and Biggs "Ron King", after being issued with false passports, and the pair also undertook expensive and painful plastic surgery to alter their facial appearances. Biggs and Flowers re-united in Sydney, where they were joined later by their wives and families.

A tip-off that police they were aware of their presence in Australia, persuaded the "Furmigens" (the Biggs' latest name change), to move to Melbourne. By then Charmain was pregnant with Farley, and the pressure on the fugitive family mounted after photographs of Biggs began to appear in Australian newspapers.

...Charmain persuaded her then 40-year-old husband to flee on his own to another safe haven.

By then the police had targeted Melbourne as the family's new hideaway, and in 1969 Charmain persuaded her then 40-year-old husband to flee on his own to another safe haven. Shortly after Ronnie absconded, police swooped on the Biggs' Melbourne home and arrested Charmain. Biggs then laid low in a Dandenong Ranges hideaway, but the net was rapidly tightening around the long term escapee, for on 27th September Eric Flowers was arrested in Sydney.

Charmain's newspaper revelations about their lives on the run funded Ronnie's next dash for freedom. Using a friend's passport, the elusive fugitive boarded the "Elloris", a Greek ship that arrived in Panama in February 1970. From there Biggs made his way to Brazil with only $200 in his pocket. As usual, however, the consummate "con man" fell on his feet in Rio de Janeiro, as within six months Ronald Biggs had found employment, a home and a new girlfriend.

However soon the indulgent life-style enjoyed by Biggs fell apart. He received the horrific news from Australia that his family had been involved in a road accident. Charmain and Farley were left relatively unscathed, but another son, Nicky, received fatal injuries. It took all the skills and attention of Xiu-Xiu, (yet another girlfriend), to restore a grieving Biggs back to his customary state of ebullient good health.

Ronnie was just starting a series of lucrative newspaper revelations in Rio de Janeiro, when another unexpected development occurred. Superintendent Jack Slipper from the London Metropolitan Flying Squad arrived in the carnival city. His presence was potentially bad news, as he had come to Rio to take Ronnie back to custody in England.

...accused of conspiring to kidnap a Brazilian citizen.

Lady luck again smiled on the celebrity fugitive however, as the working relationship between Slipper and his Brazilian counterpart, Carlos Alberto Garcia, rapidly deteriorated. Formalities of extradition became prolonged, and, after yet another shouting match, Garcia had the Slipper contingent handcuffed. They were then accused of conspiring to kidnap a Brazilian citizen.

Biggs, however, appeared destined to be returned to an English gaol, until he discovered a possible loophole from another remand prisoner. Ronnie's lover Xiu Xiu had fallen pregnant, and if her condition resulted in Biggs' fathering a Brazilian child, he would never legally have to leave his adopted country. By then a noisy majority of Rio citizens were supporting Ronnie in his fight against "Jack Slipup", and the chastened superintendent was forced to return to London without his quarry.

Charmain and the children, thanks once more to the generosity of the Australian print media, were able to visit Ronnie and his new son Michael de Castro Biggs in Rio while Xiu Xiu pursued a burgeoning career in Europe as an exotic dancer. However after his family returned to Australia, Biggs realised that he was now virtually a prisoner in Brazil. Increasingly his life became devoted to boozing, taking illicit drugs and posing for paid photographs with curious tourists.

...his life became devoted to boozing, taking illicit drugs and posing for paid photographs with curious tourists.

Meanwhile by February 1981, a bizarre kidnapping plan was being hatched by a group of six entrepreneurs in London. John Miller, Fred Prime, Patrick King, Mark Algate, Tony Marriage and Ray Jarrett decided to ingratiate them selves with Biggs in Rio before hijacking him to nearby Barbados. This Caribbean country, (unlike Brazil), had an extradition agreement with Britain. A grateful British government, they believed, would reward them handsomely for facilitating

Ronald Biggs

...forcibly abducted Biggs, and within 16 seconds he had been bundled into a car...

the return of Ronald Biggs to the English penal system.

By March Marriage and King had linked up with Biggs in Rio, where they lavishly entertained the fugitive in many local nightclubs and bars. Then, on 16th March, near the resort area of Sugar Loaf, Algate, Marriage and King forcibly abducted Biggs, and within 16 seconds he had been bundled into a car driven by Prime.

The six day sea journey on "Nowcam II" to Barbados then began, and when they berthed at the island's capital of Bridgetown, a huge group of media and government representatives were there to meet them. Again public sentiment strongly supported Biggs, and both the Brazilian and British officials diplomatically decided to allow the Barbados Government to decide on his fate. After three court hearings, Biggs was released in April to the Brazilian Embassy, from where he was flown back to Rio.

By 2001 the fugitive's health had noticeably declined, and Biggs elected to return to the care of prison hospitals back in England. The popular rogue, who had eluded the law for over 30 years in various countries, had finally decided to end his decades of life on the run.

ESCAPE LEADS TO THE GALLOWS

Ronald Ryan

The Mayor of Hawthorn was far from impressed when his daughter married Ronald Joseph Ryan, a small-time criminal and itinerant worker. His fears appeared justified when his son-in law, and then father of three, was sent to Bendigo Prison in 1960, after being convicted of factory-breaking and stealing.

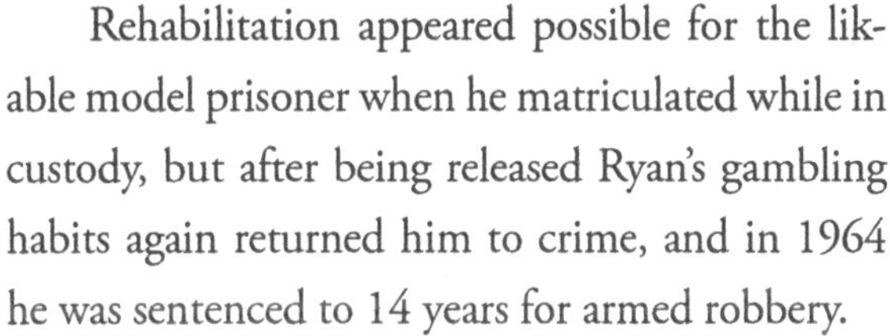

Rehabilitation appeared possible for the likable model prisoner when he matriculated while in custody, but after being released Ryan's gambling habits again returned him to crime, and in 1964 he was sentenced to 14 years for armed robbery.

In Pentridge Gaol, Ryan discovered that his wife was filing for divorce, so he decided to escape from prison and take his family to the safe haven of Brazil, which had no extradition treaty with Australia.

...a loud whip-like crack of a single shot was heard...

On 19th December 1965, Ryan and car-thief Peter John Walker escaped from the bluestone prison, after Ryan overpowered prison guard Helmut Lange and took his rifle. Bedlam broke out when the alarm was sounded, with armed wardens appearing on prison walls and guard towers, as well as in the outside streets.

In this noisy and confusing scene, a loud

whip-like crack of a single shot was heard, and George Hodson, the prison officer who was closing in on the fleeing Walker, fell to the ground. He had been fatally shot by a single bullet that travelled from the front of his body to the back, in a downward trajectory.

...a man was shot dead by Walker in a nearby public toilet.

Ryan and Walker successfully eluded their pursuers outside the prison walls in the streets of Coburg, and escaped in a car they commandeered. Soon after, while the pair was attending a private party in Melbourne, a man was shot dead by Walker in a nearby public toilet. He was later charged with manslaughter, after successfully claiming self defence.

The two escapees first hid out in country Victoria, but on January 2nd, 1966 they drove to Sydney. There they linked up with Lennie McPherson, the "Mr. Big" of crime in the harbour city. McPherson promised to help the pair to flee to Brazil, but the longstanding police informer never really intended to aid their escape.

Instead McPherson tipped off his police contact, Detective Inspector Ray "Gunner" Kelly. He secretly followed the movements of the wanted men before setting a trap, and on the evening of 6th January, Ryan and Walker were separately arrested outside Concord Hospital.

They were extradited back to Melbourne,

and jointly tried for the murder of George Hodson. Ryan's defence counsel argued that ballistics evidence indicated the perpetrator would have needed to be much taller that Ryan, according to the angle that the bullet entered the victim's body. The prosecution's responding view was that Hodson may well have been running in a stooped position, before he was fatally shot.

...Hodson may well have been running in a stooped position, before he was fatally shot.

Another prison warden, Robert Paterson, testified in court that when he was standing on a wall outside the prison, he fired a shot at the fleeing Ryan. Fourteen other witnesses testified that they only heard one shot, which appeared to cast doubts about Ryan's guilt.

The all male jury, however, found Ryan guilty of murdering George Hodson, and Justice John Starke imposed the mandatory death sentence, while Walker received a 12 year period in custody for manslaughter.

Since 1951, thirty-five other death penalty cases in Victoria had been commuted to life imprisonment. According to one juror's later account of what transpired in the group's discussions, not one of the 12 members actually believed that the death penalty would really be enacted on Ryan.

A secret eleventh-hour plea for mercy in petitioning letters was made to the Victorian governor by four of the jurors. They stated that at the time they believed the death penalty had been abolished in the state, and requested Ryan's death sentence be commuted.

The four jurors pleaded their case after it became apparent that the then Victorian Premier, Mr. (later Sir Henry) Bolte fully intended to proceed with the execution. As Ryan's appointment with the gallows drew near, several public protests were staged around the country. Melbourne newspapers, that had traditionally supported the Bolte government, deserted Sir Henry on this issue.

...a warden committed suicide by shooting himself in the head while he was on duty at Pentridge.

Some believed that Bolte was still smarting from the fact that legal manoeuvres had thwarted the 1962 execution of another convicted murderer in Peter Tait. The Premier was determined to reassert his political authority with the Ryan case.

All calls for clemency, petitions and protests were to no avail, as Ronald Ryan was hanged in "D" Division in Pentridge Prison at 8am on Friday 3rd February, 1967. About 3,000 protesters held a vigil outside the prison, and Ryan was later buried in an unmarked grave within the gaol premises.

There were two later developments that supported Ryan's consistent claims of innocence. Two years after the hanging, a warden committed suicide by shooting himself in the head while he was on duty at Pentridge. The perpetrator was Helmut

Lange, the prison officer that Ryan had overwhelmed and disarmed during the 1965 escape.

An anonymous close friend of Lange's, claimed that the warden had been a troubled man since the Ryan-Walker break-out, and confided that he had found a missing bullet casing in the prison guard tower. Lange allegedly made an official report about his discovery to prison authorities at the time, and attached the missing bullet casing. "Someone" ordered him, however, to exclude any reference about his discovery, and in court Lange testified that he did not see a bullet casing.

Seventeen years later Doug Pascoe, another prison officer, confessed that he had fired the shot that may have accidentally killed Hodson during the 1965 escape bid. Pascoe did not come forward earlier with his revelation, because at that time he was "a 23-year-old coward". His 1986 claims were discredited by authorities.

Recently Ryan's family members requested that his body be exhumed and placed beside the grave of his late wife at Portland Cemetery in the state's south-west. Then Premier John Brumby supported this step, but the daughter of the deceased Hodson vigorously opposed such a change. She maintained that Ryan did not deserve to be buried on sacred ground, and when the woman visited his unmarked grave at Pen-

...when the woman visited his unmarked grave at Pentridge, she danced and jumped on the place of burial.

tridge, she danced and jumped on the place of burial.

NO GAOL WAS "FOX" PROOF

The media in general, and police forces in three states, dubbed Russell Cox (aka Melville Peter Schnitzerling) "Mad Dog", but he was neither mad nor a "dog" (prison jargon for an informer). Men who did hard time with him at maximum security prisons such as Grafton, Katingal, Jika Jika and Pentridge's "H" Division, respectfully referred to Russell Cox as "The Fox".

His long list of escapes began at Sydney's Long Bay Prison on 8th August, 1975. Three prisoners, Allan McDougall, Marko Motic and Russell "The Fox" Cox, who were all serving time for armed robbery, used a 0.25 calibre Beretta pistol that had been smuggled into the jail, to overpower the prison guards on duty.

...used a 0.25 calibre Beretta pistol that had been smuggled into the jail, to overpower the prison guards on duty.

Prison Officer (PO) Paul Café was dragged from a nearby delivery truck and taken hostage, while PO Sam Pavich was forced at gunpoint to open the weapons cabinet. While McDougall grabbed two Smith & Wesson 0.38s, Motic and Cox positioned Café on the bonnet of the truck as a human shield, so wardens would be unable to fire shots at the vehicle. Shots were exchanged with the tower officers, however, when Cox began to drive the truck away, and the trio's freedom became short-lived.

With the protection of their exposed hostage, the fleeing prisoners successfully proceeded to a boom gate that led to the safety of Anzac Parade, but there the truck was rammed by a bread van. After another hail of bullets blew out the tyres of the truck, the three escapees and their hostage continued to flee on foot. However McDougall was the only one of the quartet not seriously wounded, when another burst of gunfire ended the escape attempt.

...bleeding profusely when gaol wardens dumped them on to the floors of nearby cells, and they were virtually left to die.

Both Cox and Motic were bleeding profusely when gaol wardens dumped them on to the floors of nearby cells, and they were virtually left to die. The jail population soon heard of their inmate's plight, and an ultimatum was issued to gaol authorities – provide immediate medical care to the two seriously wounded prisoners, or the whole institution would "blow up".

Fortunately a riot was averted when prison authorities reluctantly allowed a nursing sister and doctor to treat Cox and Motic, and the pair was transferred to Prince Henry Hospital for urgent surgery. Shortly after they were moved first to Grafton Gaol, and in 1976 to the newly constructed "escape proof" Katingal Special Security Unit. Many notorious recent escapees, including Raymond John Denning, were also in custody at Katingal.

A future mass escape plan soon evolved, and Cox was secretly provided with a piece of hacksaw blade. "The Fox" used it to cut through one of the bars in the exercise yard, and he then put his own escape plan into operation.

...but it was too late. "The Fox" had escaped from the escape-proof Katingal Unit.

On November 4th 1977, Cox asked the duty warden if he could retrieve his shoes from the exercise yard. There he jammed a paddle tennis bat into the crevice of the wall, and shimmied up the cut bar. After pulling it away, he squeezed through the caged ceiling of the exercise yard, and climbed down off the roof. As he scaled the 4.5 metre barbed wire topped perimeter fences that surrounded Katingal, Cox was spotted, but it was too late. "The Fox" had escaped from the escape-proof Katingal Unit.

The now celebrity criminal made his way first to Melbourne, and by 1978 Russell Cox was working as a seaman in England. In 1980 he moved to Germany for another two years, before returning to Victoria, where this quiet living master of disguises became a builder's labourer.

In July 1988 Cox's ex-Katingal inmate, Raymond Denning, escaped from the Goulburn Correctional Centre. Soon after he used the Katingal "old boy" network to fulfil a wish that

Queensland, NSW and Victorian Police Forces had failed to achieve for ten years, eight months and 19 days: on July 22nd 1988, Raymond Denning established contact with Australia's most wanted fugitive, Russell "The Fox" Cox.

Raymond Denning

The re-union was short lived, as Cox, Denning and later Denning's girlfriend Ann Denton, were captured after a shoot-out with police at Melbourne's Doncaster Shopping Centre, where the group was allegedly planning an armed robbery.

Six months after their capture Denning "rolled over" and became a "supergrass" or police informer to the NSW police department, in exchange for immunity from prosecution for the many serious crimes he had committed. Denning revealed to authorities the network that was spawned within Katingal, which virtually destroyed this service from the inside. Although he was released from prison after serving 19 years, the habitual criminal self-destructed, as he died shortly afterwards from a heroin overdose.

...captured after a shoot-out with police at Melbourne's Doncaster Shopping Centre

Cox finally faced trial at Sydney District Court for the 1977 Katingal escape. However in a bizarre twist, the trial judge directed the jury to acquit Cox because the Crown was unable to prove that he had been in lawful custody at the time of the escape.

It emerged that the Katingal Special Unit,

...pedantic example of legalese logic, Russell Cox escaped from a prison that never was a prison!

which was closed down seven months after Cox escaped, had never been gazetted as a prison. Furthermore there had never been any lawful warrant for the transfer of any prisoner into the building during its existence. Therefore, according to this pedantic example of legalese logic, Russell Cox escaped from a prison that never was a prison!

The semantics of the situation finally did not assist Cox who served a long gaol sentence before he was released from Grafton gaol in 2004. In his later years in custody, "The Fox" became a model prisoner, and it is now believed that Russell Cox and his partner are living and working in Queensland.

VILLAIN WHO BECAME A "MAN OF PEACE"

Gregory David Roberts, who was born in 1952, has lived a life of incredible diversity. From the 1970s until the late 1990s, he was an armed robber, prisoner, gaol escapee and an international criminal and fugitive. Since 1997 this "Jekyll and Hyde" type character has become a novelist, short story writer, poet, screenplay writer, philosopher and philanthropist.

The criminal years of Roberts' life can possibly be attributed to heroin addiction. When

Gregory Roberts

he was an addict in the 1970s, Roberts used a toy pistol to stage armed robberies of building society branches, credit unions and shops, and following his arrest he was sentenced to 19 years imprisonment.

However in July 1980 Roberts brazenly escaped in broad daylight from a Victorian maximum security prison, and became one of Australia's most wanted men. During his many years on the run, he lived briefly in New Zealand, and he then resided in India for a decade. Around the Bombay or Mumbai area, Roberts reportedly became involved with the local underworld, but in 1990 he was captured and imprisoned in Frankfurt.

...escaped in broad daylight from a Victorian maximum security prison, and became one of Australia's most wanted men.

From Germany he was extradited to Australia, where he served an additional six years in prison, including two in solitary confinement. By 1997 the now drug-free Roberts was released, and since then he has made a welcome transformation to his life.

Soon after re-joining main stream society, Roberts began working on his novel "Shantaram", which means "man of peace". This novel, which is based on the author's experiences, has since become the title for a movie, and it was Roberts who wrote the screenplay.

Gregory Roberts now has his own author's website, and he is believed to have returned to

Brenden Abbott

Mumbai, where he has reportedly established charitable foundations to assist the city's poor health care practices.

THE DROP IN BANDIT

"He never left anything to chance," recalled Detective-Sergeant Charlie Barham, with grudging admiration. "He'd have made a good cop."

This tribute was made about Brenden James Abbott, sometimes known as "the drop in bandit". Abbott was accused of 70 armed robberies that mostly centred on banks, and it is believed that he probably stole around $5,000,000 in total. Ironically the public costs that were associated with Abbott's custodial sentences and manhunts, possibly doubled that huge sum of money.

...his sentence was extended after he took a prison officer hostage during a prison riot.

As a child, Abbott endured a dysfunctional home life in both Melbourne and Alice Springs, before he was first arrested at the age of 11. In his young adult years, he served 22 months in gaol for theft, and briefly turned away from crime after being released, when he worked as a builder's labourer. After re-offending Abbott served six years in Fremantle Gaol, where his sentence was extended after he took a prison officer hostage during a prison riot.

However in November 1989, Brenden Abbott

scaled the five metre prison wall and escaped. Next day he robbed a bank, after dropping down from a hole in the roof and threatening the surprised bank staff. This was the robbery that resulted in Abbott being dubbed "the drop in bandit".

...robbed a bank, after dropping down from a hole in the roof...

Brenden Abbott proved difficult to catch. He had no drug or alcohol problems, he did not socialise in criminal circles, he was highly mobile and he was a master of disguise. By 1996 Abbott had been on the run for nearly six years, and he continued to successfully rob banks. The armed robbery of the Broadbeach branch of the Commonwealth Bank netted him $787,252, but in March 1996 "the drop in bandit" was arrested.

Tight security surrounded Abbott's court appearance, and on 6th June 1996 he was sentenced to nine years in gaol. This custodial sentence was extended to over 30 years in Queensland's penal system, when Brenden Abbott pleaded guilty to two additional armed robberies.

Over time the normally strict surveillance at the Sir David Longland maximum security gaol became more relaxed, and Abbott was able to establish a friendship with Brendan Berichon, a 20-year-old soon-to-be released armed robber and drug addict. After he walked free on 17th September 1997, Berichon enlisted the help of outside criminals to collect a .22 calibre pistol with a silencer, an AK-47 semi-automatic rifle, bolt cutters, clothing and cash, all of which were needed for Abbott's escape plan.

Angel wire hardened with diamonds, was smuggled into the gaol premises by a prisoner's girlfriend.

Within the gaol, "the drop in bandit" recruited three convicted murderers and a rapist to join him in the bid for freedom. The three murderers were 20-year-old Andrew John Jeffrey, 21-year-old Oliver Alincic and 37-year-old Jason John Nixon, while the convicted rapist was Peter Thomas Stirling.

Angel wire hardened with diamonds, which would cut through most surfaces, was smuggled into the gaol premises by a prisoner's girlfriend. The creative Abbott decided to use the backs of plastic chairs joined together to scale the razor wire fence, and hoped that tied sheets would enable them to climb up and over the prison wall. The escape date was set for November 4th 1997, when an outside team would be waiting at 11.30 pm for the escapees in a white Ford Fairlane sedan and another getaway car.

The wall scaling plan was successful, and with the aid of covering gunfire aimed at prison guards, the group was able to cut through the outer fence with bolt cutters that had been thrown over the interior fence. The dash for the cars then followed, with Abbott absconding in the Fairlane. An investigation later undertaken by the Mengler Report revealed many inadequacies in the gaol's security, and some members of the Corrective Services Executive were replaced.

Stirling was arrested with a prostitute within 48 hours at Mermaid Beach...

The day after the escape, a cheeky written memo was found in Abbott's empty cell. An application for transfer form was endorsed with the fugitive's signature as the "approving officer", and a smiley face sticker was attached to the form.

Two of Abbott's fellow escapees were not smiling for long, for they were soon returned to custody. Stirling was arrested with a prostitue within 48 hours at Mermaid Beach, and Alicic was detained soon after at Nimbin.

Nine days after the break-out Abbott and Nixon robbed the Palm Beach branch of the Commonwealth Bank, but a week later Nixon's taste of freedom ended. The convicted murderer was reaching for a shotgun near his bed, before police overpowered him. They had come across the escapee and his girlfriend in a Gold Coast resort unit by accident, when they were following up a suspected drug case.

On 30th November Andrew Jeffrey was relatively safe in a Footscray hotel in Melbourne, before a heavy drinking session brought him undone. After boasting to other drinkers about his exploits, he became involved in a brawl outside the premises, and was arrested by police before his identity had been established.

Police were aware that Abbott and Berichon were travelling together, but as weeks went by no authentic sightings of the two fugitives were reported. Though the Queensland Government offered a generous reward for their re-capture, Abbott used his clever disguises to still travel interstate. A DNA reading confirmed that the Perth suburban bank robbery on 19th December 1997, was committed by "the drop in bandit.".

...the young, heavy drug user unwittingly exposed the where-abouts of the master escape artist.

The fugitive pair based themselves for most of those months on the run at a Nicholson street flat, in the Melbourne suburb of Carlton. With them was Berichon's Thai prostitute girlfriend, Ruang Khiankham ("Michelle"), who was an illegal immigrant.

Abbott's choice of Berichon as a companion was inherently risky, and on 20th April 1998, the young, heavy drug user unwittingly exposed the whereabouts of the master escape artist. When Berichon approached a dealer in the Melbourne suburb of Box Hill that day, he was unaware that he was being observed. Two policemen drove towards the dealer and Berichon, and while being questioned, the wanted man produced a 9mm pistol and wounded both officers.

The desperate fugitive then forced a

56-year-old woman at gunpoint to drive him back to Carlton, and the trio fled just before police raided their flat. They drove to Adelaide, where they split up, before agreeing to rendezvous later in Darwin.

Marijuana, firearms and disguises were found in a nearby Land cruiser...

The net was now closing in, and police became aware that Abbott was driving towards Darwin in a stolen Landcruiser. On 2nd May 1998, a casually dressed and strongly built man was arrested at gunpoint, after washing clothes at a Darwin laundromat. Marijuana, firearms and disguises were found in a nearby Land cruiser, and the apprehended man was identified as Brenden Abbott.

Among the fugitive's possessions was a wallet that contained details about the Luma Luma accommodation apartments, and a telephone number was scratched into the leather of the wallet. Police used this number to inform Berichon that he was surrounded, after enquiries revealed that a man and an Asian woman were staying in room 608 at Luma Luma. Berichon knew he was trapped, and he surrendered quietly, after ensuring the arrested Michelle was unharmed.

Abbott was flown back to Brisbane under heavily armed escort, Berichon was extradited to Melbourne, and "Michelle" was deported back to

It may be one of the few pleasures that the "drop in bandit" experiences for the next three decades.

Thailand. Both Abbott and Berichon are serving long custodial sentences, and police believe that "the drop on bandit" will "do his time hard" over the next 30 years.

Already he has lodged complaints about his treatment in gaol, but there were no complaints from Abbott when a 46-year-old mother of six "put something into Brenden's life" by unexpectedly exposing her body to him during a custodial visit.

It may be one of the few pleasures that the "drop in bandit" experiences for quite some time.

FUGITIVE LOVERS

Heather Parker had been a prison warden for three years before she met hardened criminal Peter Gibb at the Melbourne Remand Centre. Parker's own marriage was on shaky ground, and she soon became attracted to the cocky, well built 38-year-old inmate.

The 27-year-old smitten woman seemed oblivious to Gibb's violent history. Gibb had been a career criminal since his teen-age years, and his offences included manslaughter and armed robbery convictions. He was currently likely to commence a 12-year sentence

Her workmates' feelings towards their budding romance were hostile, especially when

Parker and Gibb were spotted sneaking into a broom cupboard together. The wardens staged a stop work meeting, and their protest resulted in Parker being transferred, first to the security ward at St. Vincent's Hospital, and then to a clerical position at head office. Concerns were again expressed, when Parker was observed in an area there that contained internal security reports.

At that time, Gibb and 40-year-old Archie Butterly, another habitual criminal, were planning an escape, and Parker readily agreed to assist them. She persuaded underworld contact Alex Thompson to steal a station wagon, a four-wheel-drive vehicle, and some false number plates.

Parker obtained an automatic pistol and three stun guns from USA by mail order. The four-wheel drive was then fitted out with camping gear, food supplies, mobile phones, bolt cutters, handcuffs and a camouflage net.

Parker obtained an automatic pistol and three stun guns from USA by mail order.

The break-out occurred ten days after Gibb was sentenced. At six pm on Sunday March 2nd, an explosion rocked the Remand Centre. Gibb and Butterly smashed a window and used tied sheets to shimmy down the wall into nearby La Trobe Street where a Ford Falcon was parked ready for their use.

The escape was successful, but not without mishaps, altercations and accidents. Butterly was quite badly injured when their car crashed as the fugitives fled, Gibb had his arm broken by a police baton, and a senior constable was wounded in the same incident.

After rendezvousing with Parker at Frankston, the trio switched over to the stolen four-wheel-drive vehicle, and drove towards the rural area of Gippsland. At the Latrobe Regional Hospital in Moe, Butterly received medical attention before Gibb drove towards more remote areas in the state's north-east.

As police dogs began tracking nearby, shots rang out and a gun battle was waged.

They ended their first full day of freedom at the Gaffney Creek Hotel, a historic building that was built in 1865. That night Gibb entertained some locals with a few songs on his guitar, but the fugitives inexplicably turned nasty after vacating the premises around 1am. The room they booked was set on fire, and the heritage building was burnt to the ground.

News of the fire brought police rushing to the area, and an intensive search began. At noon on 13th March the stolen blue Pajero was found concealed in ferns near Picnic Point, about 25 kilometres from Gaffney Creek. As police dogs began tracking nearby, shots rang out and a gun battle was waged.

Before long Parker and Gibb was cornered waist -deep in the Goulburn River. An aggressive

Parker strongly resisted arrest, but Gibb passively surrendered himself to police.

Nearby was the body of Archie Butterly with a bullet wound behind his left ear. To this day it is not clear who killed the escapee, but gunshot residue found on Parker's hand at the time of arrest, suggest it may have been she who fired the fatal shot. The weapon used was the revolver that had been stolen by Gibb from Senior Constable Treloar, during their struggle on the day of the break-out.

On Monday 15th March, Gibb and Parker were charged with six counts of attempted murder and 23 other counts. Both received ten years imprisonment, with Parker's non-parole period being six years and six months, while Gibb was not eligible for release under eight years. Parker's sentence was then reduced further on appeal, and she actually spent only three months on remand at Barwon Prison, before being released to care for her mother

In their court appearance, the pair showed every indication of being deeply in love, and a psychiatrist who examined Parker maintained that she was motivated by "a pathological infatuation". Since serving their time, the couple have lived together in suburban Melbourne, but their relationship has sadly deteriorated. On September 3rd 2004 Heather Parker faced a pre-trial sentence hearing for bashing a woman who required

...she was motivated by "a pathological infatuation".

hospital treatment for six days.

The victim had slept with Peter Gibb and Parker kicked, punched and clubbed her rival brutally.

By then Gibb had served several more gaol sentences, and he has frequently assaulted Parker in drunken attacks. Peter Gibb died on 23 January 2011 after being beaten by three men in his home a week earlier.

"PRISONS WITHIN PRISONS" – A SHAMEFUL ERA

High security risk prisoners, such as Cox, Denning and Abbott, present a constant challenge to governments and prison authorities. During the 1970–80s the need for a more secure deterrent for serial escapees, led to the construction of "escape proof gaols within gaols" such as Jika Jika and Katingal.

...four prisoners also broke out of the "escape proof" Jika Jika in 1983.

At its time Jika Jika (also called the K Division High Security Unit), that was situated within Melbourne's Pentridge Prison, was considered to be a "state of the arts" construction for Victoria's hardest and longest serving prisoners. The strongly constructed building received the "Excellence in Concrete Award" from the Concrete Institute of Australia.

The design was based on the idea of six separate units at the end of radiating spines. The unit comprised electronic doors, closed circuit TV and remote locking. Furnishings were sparse, and prisoners exercised in aviary-like escape proof yards. It was a climate controlled division that was devoid of any fresh air circulation.

Overall units such as Jika Jika and Sydney's Katingal complex, aimed to keep staff costs to a minimum, and security to a maximum. Russell Cox did escape from Katingal in 1977, and four prisoners also broke out of the "escape proof" Jika Jika in 1983.

By then the harsh conditions under which prisoners lived, was being criticised by many civil rights supporters, and in 1987 a protest was initiated within Jika Jika that resulted in tragic consequences.

Inmates Robert Wright, Jimmy Loughnan, Arthur Gallagher, David McGauley and Ricky Morris (from one side of the unit), along with "Jenny" Craig Minogue and three other inmates on the other side, sealed off their section doors with a tennis net. Mattresses and other bedding were then stacked against the doors, and the windows in the day room were covered with paper, so that prison officers could not identify which prisoners caused the ensuring damage.

Plumbing was torn from the walls to enable the prisoners to breathe when they set the unit on fire.

Plumbing was torn from the walls to enable the prisoners to breathe when they set the unit on fire. However the toxic black smoke that billowed from the fire, proved too much for Wright, Loughlan, Gallagher, McGauley and Morris, and all five perished in the fire. Minogue, the convicted Russell Street bomber, and the three other inmates, all survived.

Robert Wright's sister became one of the unit's most vocal public critics, and before long Jim Kennan, who was then Victorian Attorney General and Minister for Corrections, ordered the closure of Jika Jika.

Katingal had been previously closed in 1978.

CHAPTER THIRTEEN:

WHERE ARE YOU?

Each year in Australia around 30,000 missing persons are reported to police and welfare agencies, which is a rate of one person being unaccounted for every 18 minutes.

This depressing statistic exceeds the total number of victims reported to police for homicides, sexual assaults and armed robbery combined.

Nationally, the number of missing people reported to police is around 1.55 per thousand. Rates vary considerably around the country, with South Australia and the Australian Capital Territory (ACT) having rates that are double the national average. Both these areas, it should be noted, use different statistical techniques from the other states and territories.

Research also shows that the trauma flow on from disappearances is highly significant. An average of 12 people are affected by the stress of not knowing where their missing loved ones are located. Overall the financial burden to taxpayers is considerable, with approximately $2,400 being outlaid in search costs, loss of earnings while people search, and associated legal costs, for every missing person.

Fortunately nearly all missing individuals are found, with around 86% being located within a week, usually at a friend's home or with friends. Often the missing person contacts home themselves, or is discovered within two days by family or friends, rather than by police.

Over Christmas and New Year there is a sharp rise in the number of parental abductions...

Missing person reports includes a significant proportion of people who have disappeared from an institution of some kind. These include psychiatric and general hospitals, support accommodation for the aged and intellectually disabled, or youth supervised care and detention facilities.

In indigenous communities, there are a disturbingly large number of young females represented in the statistics. In 2002 there were 133 files of missing aboriginal women, and almost 50% of these were aged between 12 and 15.

Over Christmas and New Year there is a sharp rise in the number of parental abductions, and on average two-three children are illegally taken out of the country each year by one of the parents.

Unemployed people are strongly represented among the missing, and over 30% of those being sought are repeat offenders. In the majority of cases the missing person was last seen at home during daylight hours, and Friday is the most common day of the week for people to go missing.

Friday is the most common day of the week for people to go missing.

A TRAGIC CASE STUDY – RED NOT THE SYMBOL FOR HAPPINESS

In Chinese culture, red is often the symbol for happiness. On Queensland's Sunshine Coast during the late 1980s and early '90s, red first became the symbol for hope, but finally for prolonged despair, after a boy wearing a red shirt vanished without trace.

On 19th December 1989, 13-year-old Daniel Morcombe waited at a bus stop close to his Palmwood home. He planned to visit the Sunshine Plaza Shopping Centre to buy Christmas presents and have a haircut. It was a routine that had passed without mishap on many occasions, but fate decreed that this day would be cruelly different.

The scheduled bus for this route had broken down, and later there were reported sightings of Daniel, still waiting patiently at the bus stop, for at least 35 minutes between

Daniel Morcombe

1.40–2.15 that afternoon.

Police believe that during that time span, two men in a blue car enticed or forced the young teenager into their vehicle and drove away. A description of a man seen at the bus stop near Daniel was soon circulated. It was reported that the suspect was aged between 25-35 years. He had a pale, gaunt face, a muscular build, and dark brown, wavy hair.

A prolonged public campaign, unprecedented in its size and scope, has since been conducted to find the missing boy. Denise and Bruce Morcombe, the parents of Daniel, raised over $100,000 for a mammoth advertising campaign in an attempt to solve their son's abduction case. Approximately another million dollars has been donated from other sources, to solve a mystery that arouses deep feelings of empathy in every parent.

...raised over $100,000 for a mammoth advertising campaign in an attempt to solve their son's abduction case.

The Daniel Morcombe mystery was screened on Channel Two's "Australian Story", and featured in the "Woman's Weekly" publication. The public responded with about 3,500 calls to Crime Stoppers. On the Sunshine Coast householders were encouraged to have red ribbons displayed conspicuously on their properties, to keep the disappearance focussed in peoples' minds.

A "Walk for Daniel Day", was organised in the local community, and 52 schools along the

Sunshine Coast conducted "Red Days". Across the entire nation, posters, banners, and bumper stickers were circulated. Halloween, celebrated on 31st October each year, was set aside along the Central Queensland coast as "The Day For Daniel".

Halloween, celebrated on 31st October each year, was set aside along the Central Queensland coast as "The Day For Daniel".

A long eight years after Daniel Morcombe's abduction, police charged Brett Peter Cowan with his murder. Cowan was found guilty and, on 13 March 2014 he was sentenced to life in prison, with a non-parole period of 20 years. Police are still baffled by the disappearance of the three Beaumont children in Adelaide on Australia Day 1966, and two decades before Daniel Morcombe vanished, there was a similar precedent, not far from that more recent abduction.

Queensland teenager Peter Austin unfortunately accepted a lift from Robin Reid and Paul Luckman in Brisbane, and the two paedophile soldiers tortured, sodomised and killed the young lad before burying him near the NSW border. Both gruesome offenders were captured and sentenced, and in custody Luckman surprisingly obtained permission to have a successful sex change operation.

...after 86 years the three siblings had a joyous reunion.

GOOD NEWS STORIES

The current world record for the longest time a family has been separated, before being reunited, is 86 years.

The Salvation Army in the UK was asked to help a woman find her family after she learned that her birth parents were itinerant actors who had three other children. First a nephew was contacted, and he was able to ring his mother and her younger sister, so after 86 years the three siblings had a joyous reunion.

Another heart warming example took 60 years before it became resolved. "Maude" was the youngest of three sisters, but as a baby she was separated from her two siblings during World War II. A welfare agency reunited the trio, even though one was living on the Gold Coast, and the other resided in the UK.

A 75-year-old English woman came to Australia on a mission to find her two half-brothers. The last known address of one was near Ballarat, and a quick search of the electoral roll showed that there was a person by that name living in the town. Soon she was talking to him by phone, and it was quickly established that they were brother and sister.

A father in South Australia contacted a welfare

agency to help find his son whom he had not seen for 25 years. Six months later the son replied to a re-directed letter, and the welfare agency informed the man that his father was looking for him.

The overjoyed son immediately purchased a train ticket to South Australia, but was unaware that his father was about to depart by bus to link up with him in Melbourne. Fortunately the father was contacted before boarding the bus, so he then waited excitedly for his long lost son to arrive.

CHAPTER 14:

CRIMES IN A TECHNOLOGICAL AGE

Advances in technology have meant that a new sort of crime has arisen – one that is facilitated by the use of computers and the internet.

The crimes themselves are much the same as they have ever been: fraud, pornography, paedophilia, theft, harassment and many others. With the exception of murder, all crimes that can be committed are helped by the new technology.

"Upskirting" and "downblousing" are two new crimes that have only come to light in the last couple of years. These crimes are hi-tech forms of "peeping toms" and are now punishable by law. In the US, the punishment is currently a year in jail. In Australia, a Japanese tourist caught upskirting at the Australian Open Tennis tournament in 2007, received a two month jail sentence.

The law has been slow to catch up with advances in technology, but it is now acting more quickly to protect people's privacy. Every state has a specific law against these crimes, which are made possible due to mobile phone cameras that are easily concealed.

In Japan, which has a huge problem with this crime, all mobile phone cameras must make an audible click when a photo is taken.

There are hundreds of sites on the internet which offer to pay for the "upskirting" and "downblousing" pictures.

Of course pornography and paedophilia have been made more easily accessible with the advent of the internet. Authorities are hampered in their quest to shut down such activities that often originate in overseas countries which do not have Australia's stringent laws.

...one in five children had been sexually approached while on the internet.

Paedophiles can use social websites to find potential victims and "groom" them for further contact. Children can be lured into private chat rooms where they can be exposed to lewd images that flick up onto their screens, before they realise what has happened. Many children evidently do not report such incidents, as they somehow feel that it is their fault.

Statistics from the US in 2006 found that one in five children had been sexually approached while on the internet. One in four had been exposed to inappropriate images. It is supposed that statistics in Australia would be very similar.

Fraud crimes, such as the infamous Nigerian Scam, continue to trick people. In 1997 in the US it was estimated that $100 million was scammed from unwitting victims. In 2007 the amount had risen to $198 million – up 8% since 2005.

The scam involves the victim sending bank details to a foreign country, so that a foreigner can deposit money from his country before moving it elsewhere, with the promise of a percentage of it being given to the victim. The reasons for having to move the money through a foreign bank vary, but the lure of millions of dollars for a seemingly small task, blinds the victims to the danger of the fraud.

The scam involves the victim sending bank details to a foreign country...

This type of scam has been going on since the 1920s, when perpetrators used written letters before graduating to faxes and now emails. The authentic Central Bank of Nigeria has been embarrassed by this fraud, and has even placed advertisements in newspapers warning people against the scam. Of course the email need not mention Nigeria, as they can come from any number of other countries. Some, for example, have originated from Sierra Leone or the Ivory Coast.

In Australia the Australian Competition and Consumer Commission released "The Little Black Book of Scams" in 2008 to help people avoid the traps associated with scams. They also have a dedicated website www.scamwatch.gov.au to alert people about the latest examples of this pernicious form of criminal activity.

Privacy is a big issue for users of the internet. Hacking is a term used to denote the illegal entry into a computer's hard drive in order to change and/or gain access to information, or to disable the computer's hard drive. It has exposed individuals, companies, and even government bodies, with the nightmare of having files stolen. The confidential information thus gained, can either be used against them, or published in the wider community, in order to embarrass or defame.

In 1989 two Australian males became the first hackers.

In 1989 two Australian males became the first hackers. They were convicted of various offences. One of them, who went by the pseudonym of "Electron", pleaded guilty to 14 offences, and in June 1993 was given a suspended six-month jail sentence and 300 hours community service. "Phoenix", the other Australian hacker, was put on a $1000 good-behaviour bond and given a 12 month suspended sentence and 500 hours community service. Since then many people have been convicted of computer-related crimes.

Federal Police believe it is only a matter of time before hacking will cause death...

The amount of hacking into US defence systems increased during the Gulf War of 1991. Federal Police believe it is only a matter of time before hacking will cause death, with bombs being involved and real people being targeted.

The rise of this crime has meant that users of the internet are now aware of the risks that hacking presents. Many companies sell anti-virus, anti-spyware and similar software, in an effort to protect users' systems.

Hacking is not only the province of private individuals. Countries have been found trying to hack into other countries' computer networks in order to find out classified information, such as military secrets.

In February 2008, it was alleged that the Chinese Government had unsuccessfully tried to hack into the Australian Government's computer network in order to find out military secrets, prices that Australians would ask for their natural resources, and intelligence received from other countries.

Intelligence sources at the time said," Espionage over the internet is a major battleground of the future." (The Age, Feb 10, 2008)

Examples of other computer crimes involved with the use of the internet include: "dumping", or getting people to transfer to a more expensive telephone connection without their knowledge, and "phishing". This is another form of computer crime which attempts to get sensitive information, such as usernames, passwords and credit card details, by pretending to be a bank or some other financial institution.

Criminals will always exploit what society uses.

Cyber bullying is an invidious escalation from the usual bullying that goes on behind the shelter shed in school-grounds. With the use of mobile phones to send disturbing messages or images, and using chat rooms to disseminate hurtful comments about the victim, technology has raised the stakes in this nasty practice.

Criminals will always exploit what society uses. Technology, in the hands of those in the know, extends the parameters of what can be achieved by the criminal classes. Police have the responsibility to remain at the forefront of technological advances in order to keep ahead of the crimes that can be committed in a technological age.

In Queensland the police have been equipped with the latest technology to fight crime. Victoria Police maintain they have the reputation as a premier policing service, due to major developments of technology in forensics and communications. In NSW the Special Services Group is a highly technical component of their Police Force, which enables lawful investigations through technology.

In September 2007, the Tasmanian Police Force publicised details about the advanced technology they had purchased for forensic photography.

Other Australian states and territories have their own methods for combating crimes caused by technology.

A search on books about computer crime on the internet, will turn up hundreds of hits – proof that criminals have well and truly embraced the latest in technology.

Theft on a massive scale has been made possible with the advent of technology. Even the Great Train Robbers did not get away with the massive amounts that disappeared from Barings Bank in England in 1995, or the Societe Generale Bank in France in 2008.

Theft on a massive scale has been made possible with the advent of technology.

In the case of the Barings bank fraud, Nick Leeson managed to bankrupt the bank by unauthorised trading in futures which resulted in staggering losses of approximately 860 million pounds. Leeson was sentenced to six and a half years in jail The bank has since been taken over by ING, a Dutch bank.

Jerome Kerviel is believed to be the trader behind the massive 7.1 billion pound banking fraud...

Jerome Kerviel is believed to be the trader behind the massive 7.1 billion pound banking fraud at French bank Société Générale in 2008. When Leeson heard of this fraud, he was not surprised that it happened, as he believes that rogue trading goes on all the time. He was only surprised by the amount that was stolen.

These sorts of crimes are computer generated, and it is the only way that fraud on such a massive scale could take place.

CHAPTER 15:

LONE WOLVES IN CONCRETE JUNGLES

Across the world in recent years authorities have been challenged by a rise in terrorist, extremist or so-called 'lone wolf' attacks in major cities. Not unlike the 9-11 attack in the USA in 2001 where commercial aircraft were used as virtual heat-seeking missiles, perpetrators are using cars, trucks, home-made bombs and kitchen knives to carry out unspeakable acts of violence in crowded areas.

While Australia can't yet claim to have experienced orchestrated terrorist campaigns, one off attacks by religious extremists have occurred, as have random attacks on innocent civilians doing nothing more than going about their daily working lives in their city.

THE LINDT CAFÉ SIEGE, SYDNEY

Thus began a terrifying 16.5 hour siege, transfixing a nation as the horrific pictures beamed live into Australia's, and the world's, living rooms.

At 9.41am on Monday December 15, 2014, Man Haron Monis walked into the Lindt Chocolate Café in Sydney's Martin Place, directly opposite the television studios of a national TV network, Channel 7. He had a blue sports bag over his shoulder and carried an old pump-action sawn-off shotgun. Monis disabled the automatic glass sliding doors, thereby trapping 18 hostages — eight staff and 10 customers — inside the café. He ordered Café manager Tori Johnson to call 000 and inform police that an armed Islamic State operative had taken 18 people hostage, and that other operatives, armed with bombs, were stationed at various sites around the city.

Thus began a terrifying 16.5 hour siege, transfixing a nation as the horrific pictures beamed live into Australia's, and the world's, living rooms. Monis became angry and frustrated as his demands (relayed to police command via media outlets or the social media pages of hostages) to have an ISIS flag delivered to him and to speak with the Prime Minister on live radio, were delayed or rejected. As the drama unfolded over long and stressful hours Monis became increasingly agitated and distracted, allowing brave hostages to find windows of opportunity to flee through side and front doors into the arms of the Tactical Response Unit. Monis's mood darkened even further, taking pot shots at those escaping or randomly inside the café.

Just after 2am on December 15, Monis fired a shot towards the kitchen, and police snipers were ordered to close in on the front door. At 2.14am, Monis coldly executed Tori Johnson with a shot to the back of the head, signalling the storming of the café by armed police. In the hail of bloody gunfire, 38 year old barrister Katrina Dawson was fatally wounded by a ricoching police bullet, three other hostages received gunshot wounds, and Man Monis was taken down, hit 13 times by police shots.

When police declared the siege at an end, over the ensuing days thousands of shellshocked Sydneysiders visited the site to pay their respects. The impact on the psyche of the city, and indeed all Australians, was palpable. It is estimated that more than 100,000 bouquets of flowers were laid in memory of Katrina Dawson and Tori Johnson, forming a Field of Flowers that blanketed much of Martin Place. The Lindt Café reopened in March 2015, some three months after the horrific event that will mark it in history for years to come.

THE BOURKE ST MALL CAR ATTACK, MELBOURNE

Close to three years after the Lindt Café siege, it was Melbourne CBD's turn to become the scene of a drug-fuelled, psychotic rampage — but this time the perpetrator's weapon was not a gun or a bomb, but a stolen Holden Commodore.

In the 48 hours leading up to James Gargasoulas's death-drive through the crowded Bourke St Mall on January 20, 2017 he had become violent, delusional and taken methamphetamine. On January 18, after a bizarre altercation with his mother's partner in which he burnt a bible, he punched him and stole his car. Then, in the wee hours of January 20, Gargasoulas, high on drugs, stabbed his brother in the street, leaving him with critical head and chest injuries. He later took his girlfriend hostage, released her and then proceeded on in the stolen Commodore to Melbourne's CBD.

By this stage, police were tailing Gargasoulas's movements but had not intercepted him, unaware of the despicable act that was about to unfold. The maroon Commodore circled the intersection outside busy Flinders St Station, holding up traffic with its driver screaming out of the window to stunned onlookers. Followed by several police vehicles, Gargasoulas moved slowly along Swanston St towards the Bourke St Mall.

He turned into the usually car-free mall, packed with lunchtime shoppers on what seemed to be a normal Friday afternoon. Without warning he slammed on the accelerator, mounted the footpath and in a deliberate act of unspeakable evil, mowed down innocent bystanders and pedestrians, killing 3 people at the scene and injuring 27 others before being apprehended by police in front of traumatised witnesses. Two further victims died later that day and another died 10 days later in hospital, adding a sixth charge of murder to a string of criminal offences.

...this time the perpetrator's weapon was not a gun or a bomb, but a stolen Holden Commodore.

In February 2019, Gargasoulas was jailed for a non-parole period of 46 years for the murders of Jessica Mudie (22), Yosuke Kanno (25), Matthew Poh Chuan Si (33), Bhavita Patel (33), Thalia Hakin (10) and Zachary Matthew-Bryant (3 months).

BIBLIOGRAPHY

Age Newspapers (July 2007–April 2008)

Brown, Malcolm, (editor) "Bombs, Cuts and Knives", New Holland Books, Sydney (2000).

Bowles, Robin "Rough Justice", Five Mile Press, Rowville, Victoria, (2007).

Callaghan, Greg "Bondi Badlands", Allen & Unwin, (2003)

Fife-Yeoman, Janet "Killing Jodie" Penguin Books, ((2007)

Henderson, Monika, Henderson, Peter, Kieran, Carol, Australian Institute of Criminology, no. 144, Missing Persons Incidence, Issues and Impacts

Howell, Wayne "Reasonable Doubt" Five Mile Press, Rowville, Victoria (2007

Kidd, Paul "Never to be Released" Pan McMillan, 2001

Marshall, Debi "The Devil's Garden" Random House (2007)

Shand, Adam "Big Shots", Penguin Books, Sydney (2007)

Smith, Chris "Stalked", New Holland Books, (2007)

Sylvester John and Rule Andrew, "Leadbelly" Floridale, (2004)

INDEX

K

L

M

ABOUT THE AUTHOR

Ian Ferguson is the author of nine previously published books. He has also contributed regular articles for various national magazines and regional newspapers.

Previous titles through Brolga Publishing:

2005 *A Tickle to Silly Leg: Aussie Cricket Humour*
2006 *Wearing the Baggy Green: Australian Cricket Encyclopedia*
2007 *Murders that Shocked Australia*
2007 *Wearing the Baggy Green 2nd edition*
2008 *Murders that Shocked Australia 2nd edition*

Also by Ian Ferguson

MURDERS THAT SHOCKED AUSTRALIA

Murders that Shocked Australia takes the reader through Australia's most challenging murders and personalities, from Ned Kelly to the baffling Pyjama Girl case. Enthralling and chilling at turns, this book explores the true-life cases that have gripped Australia and our media. It takes us on a trip through the human psyche, as well as exploring the darker side of what it means to be Australian.

ORDER

Crimes That Shocked Australia

Ian Ferguson

ISBN: 9781921221569

		Qty
RRP	AU$24.99	.....
Postage within Australia	AU$5.00	.....
	TOTAL* $________	

* All prices include GST

Name: ....

Address: ....

....

Phone: ....

Email: ....

Payment: [ ] Money Order [ ] Cheque [ ] MasterCard [ ]Visa

Cardholder's Name:..

Credit Card Number: ....

Signature:..

Expiry Date: ....

Allow 7 days for delivery.

Payment to: Marzocco Consultancy (ABN 14 067 257 390)
PO Box 452
Torquay Victoria 3228
Australia

Be Published

Publish through a successful publisher.
Brolga Publishing is represented through:

- National book trade distribution, including sales, marketing & distribution through Simon & Schuster.
- International book trade distribution to:
    - The United Kingdom
    - Sales representation in South East Asia
- Worldwide e-Book distribution

For details and enquiries, contact:

Brolga Publishing Pty Ltd
ABN 46 063 962 443
PO Box 452
Torquay Victoria 3228
Australia

markzocchi@brolgapublishing.com.au
(Email for a catalogue request)